Our kids are our most precious natural resource, but they are under attack today in unprecedented ways. Our kids are being picked off in sophisticated ways because parents do not know how to equip their children to face something they themselves never experienced. *ReCreate* is a survival manual for families that shows how to retake the culture, one family at a time.

DAVID BARTON
Founder and President, Wallbuilder Presentations Inc.

Ron Luce has articulated the battle cry of his heart in his great new book *ReCreate*, and I thoroughly encourage parents and grandparents of every age to act on this wonderful message. If you don't provide a dream to help shape your children's future, the selfish and destructive culture all around us surely will.

TOMMY BARNETT
Pastor, Phoenix First Assembly and Los Angeles Dream Center

Ron Luce recognizes the power of our culture and understands the urgent need to equip parents to stand firm in the fight for their families. Make no mistake: The culture war is real. But thanks to the strategic insight and principles Ron offers on these pages, we can win the victory.

JODIE BERNDT
Author, *Praying the Scriptures for Your Teenagers*

From a man who has dedicated his life to reaching our youth now comes his most significant pursuit . . . *reaching the parents*. Ron Luce stands in the valley of persuasion, throwing a rock in the minds of the giants destroying our youth.

PASTOR GLEN BERTEAU
Pastor, Calvary Temple Worship Centre

In *ReCreate*, Ron has taken a step to reach out to parents who need to understand the culture that is forming our children. With this powerful and strategic message, Ron has positioned parents to be stronger influencers in the home and raise children who stand for the purposes of God in their generation.

JOHN AND LISA BEVERE
Cofounders, Messenger International
Bestselling authors and speakers

ReCreate offers practical help and hope for parents rocked by the deceptive realities permeating the culture in which their teens live. This is an urgent call: It is about rescuing our sons and daughters . . . and our nation!

JEFF FARMER
President, Open Bible Churches
Vice Chairman, National Association of Evangelicals

When Ron Luce shared some of these principles with my congregation, it greatly challenged and motivated our people. Ron Luce is a man committed to changing the world. Let's help him do it!

DR. RONNIE W. FLOYD
Senior Pastor, First Baptist Church of Springdale and
The Church at Pinnacle Hills

Packed with current, eye-opening information for both parents and students, *ReCreate* is a wake-up call for the Body of Christ concerning the cultural war being waged for the minds and souls of this generation.

PASTOR JENTEZEN FRANKLIN
New York Times bestselling author
Senior Pastor, Free Chapel

We are now in an undeniable crisis moment. America is at the tipping point, and Ron knows that the enemy is now inside the gates. You and I must win this battle for our youth. Ron Luce's insights will be a key component in our victory.

JIM GARLOW
Pastor, Skyline Church

The best biblical example of discipleship is a parent training a child. Ron Luce writes with authority, knowledge and passion. He will give you the tools you need to secure the spiritual health of your children.

ALTON GARRISON
Assistant General Superintendent, The Assemblies of God

Culture is an inescapable influence in our lives. The question is, do we absorb it or counter it? In *ReCreate*, Ron Luce articulates a dynamic plan for confronting and changing the destructive forces of popular culture that surround our generation.

DR. JACK GRAHAM
Pastor, Prestonwood Baptist Church

Ron Luce has diagnosed the disease of our culture that is tearing at the fabric of families. Every mom and dad should read these words and apply them in raising a new generation of young people equipped to meet life's challenges with the power of the gospel.

DR. O. S. HAWKINS
President, Annuity Board of the Southern Baptist Convention

As a veteran in youth ministry and as a parent of two amazing young adult sons, I recommend *ReCreate* to anyone who doesn't want to falter in the all-important role of parenting.

JEANNE MAYO
President, Youth Leader's Coach
Youth communicator and author

This is typical Ron Luce stuff. Hard hitting, straight to the point, on the mark, and right between the eyes. Truly an important word for the day.

DR. MARK RUTLAND
Founder and president, Global Servants
President of Southeastern University

Whether you are a single adult looking to get married, the parent of a toddler, or have years of parenting experience, this book will help you regain an understanding of God's design.

ED YOUNG
Founding and Senior Pastor of Fellowship Church
Author, *Kid CEO*

RON LUCE

RE·CREATE

BUILDING A CULTURE IN YOUR HOME STRONGER THAN THE CULTURE DECEIVING YOUR KIDS

Regal

From Gospel Light
Ventura, California, U.S.A.

Published by Regal
From Gospel Light
Ventura, California, U.S.A.
www.regalbooks.com
Printed in the U.S.A.

Scripture quotations are taken from:
NIV—the *Holy Bible, New International Version*®. Copyright © 1973, 1978, 1984 by International
Bible Society. Used by permission of Zondervan Publishing House. All rights reserved.
NLT—the *Holy Bible, New Living Translation*, copyright © 1996. Used by permission of
Tyndale House Publishers, Inc., Wheaton, Illinois 60189. All rights reserved.

Library of Congress Cataloging-in-Publication Data
Luce, Ron.
Recreate : building a culture in your home stronger than the culture deceiving
your kids / Ron Luce.
p. cm.
ISBN 978-0-8307-4637-8 (hard cover)
1. Parenting—Religious aspects—Christianity. 2. Children—Religious life.
3. Christian education—Home training. I. Title.
BV4529.L85 2008
248.8'45—dc22
2008014889

1 2 3 4 5 6 7 8 9 10 11 12 13 14 15 / 15 14 13 12 11 10 09 08

Rights for publishing this book outside the U.S.A. or in non-English languages are administered
by Gospel Light Worldwide, an international not-for-profit ministry. For additional information, please visit www.glww.org, email info@glww.org, or write to Gospel Light Worldwide, 1957
Eastman Avenue, Ventura, CA 93003, U.S.A.

CONTENTS

Section I: ReCreating the Culture in Your Family

Section II: ReCreating a Culture in Your Church That Overwhelms the World

Section III: ReCreating Our Society

FOREWORD

Jack Hayford, Samuel Rodriguez and Harry Jackson

This is a book of practical insights for parents who care. And what parent doesn't care for his or her child? We all do. Anna and I have four children, all of whom are now grown and providing us with joy today—the joy of seeing them fulfilled in marriages that are working, and the joy of seeing their family, our grandchildren, happy.

None of those joys came naturally. When it comes to trying to cultivate a healthy family, too many of the trends in our world are tilted against that health. These trends are corrosive to a home where wisdom and love meet in balance and build relationships that bring parents and children into what "family" is supposed to be about.

This book will help anyone who is serious about finding his or her way toward such a family or help him or her rebuild whatever has been broken relationally. Ron Luce is writing about something that he and his wife, Katie, have learned on the best terms: *They got started* in their marriage and family with the kind of guidance you'll find here. Rebuilding wasn't needed—they just applied and stuck with what they had been taught.

But Ron isn't being preachy here about their successes. He knows, like I do, that when you find true parental wisdom and success today, it comes from a Source that moves you to sing "Amazing Grace," not "I Did It My Way." Nor is Ron unfamiliar with the challenges of rebuilding, even though that hasn't been his and Katie's task. As founder and president of

Teen Mania, he has had day-to-day contact with young people on every point of the spectrum of difficulty, from shredded family relationships to confusion over values, purpose and meaning, which so often distill from abuse, rebellion, addiction or a personal sense of futility.

I am thankful to be asked to introduce this book, and Ron, to you. If you know him, you probably didn't need my explanation—one that comes from the mix of my familiarity with his life and work for over a dozen years and my pastoral experience with thousands of parents for over 40 years.

So open the pages and proceed. Here is a handbook on holistic thinking about the children you love and who you want to see find what's best for them. As I said, it's loaded with the amazing and, I predict, can set you singing of that dimension of grace in your family as you welcome the one Source of wisdom that provides that grace. That source is the Fountainhead of help for every parent—the God who created moms, dads and kids.

Let Ron help you get a contemporary picture of how His ways work in a twenty-first-century culture—even when broken things need rebuilding.

Jack W. Hayford
Chancellor, The King's College Seminary
President, International Foursquare Churches
Founding Pastor, The Church On The Way

Is this the end of the family unit as we know it? Can the Christian family and the values-driven home survive the twenty-first-century cultural enclaves embedded in the 24-hour hyper information age? Can the Church of Jesus Christ survive without healthy marriages and family?

These questions speak to the necessity of a righteous revolution and a justice movement that will contextualize a transformational missiology that is committed to building healthy families, holy homes and holistic communities. Prior to the Church addressing and incorporating a strategic plan to reform the family unit outside the corridors of the Cathedral, we need to strengthen the families within our walls. Accordingly, Ron Luce presents a viable solution to the challenge.

Ron understands that unprecedented times require unprecedented measures. Never before has the institution of the family faced such egregious assault as we experience in our present twenty-first-century reality. Parenting strategies have surrendered to popular-culture biblical truths and precepts, thus placing the family in the midst of a tumultuous sea without any means for survival or success. Yet in the midst of this great crisis, God equips His children with the necessary acumen to counter the attacks and preserve the family unit with a biblical worldview that embraces righteousness and justice in the name of Christ. In this book, Ron Luce presets practical parenting principles that are necessary for the raising of our children and the preservation of the family unit within the framework of God's original plan.

In the midst of the MySpace, Facebook, iPod, TMZ and digital morally ambiguous culture, Ron Luce calls us not just to engage the culture but also to reform it through Christ-centered principles. This book serves as a survivor's manual for the North American family and especially for every Christian family confronting the social and moral challenges of our time. I wholeheartedly believe that at the end of the day, this book will equip the reader to articulate vociferously the declaration Joshua made before the children of Israel: "As for me and my house, we shall serve the living God."

Rev. Samuel Rodriguez
President, National Hispanic Christian Leadership Conference

The Church is in danger of being muzzled. We have been told so often what we believe is erroneous that some of us have lost the will to publicly display our faith. We are not blind to society's ills, but we feel pressured to dumb down the gospel to be more socially acceptable. Although we want to be courageous defenders of the faith, many of us are simply overwhelmed. We want to be God's ambassadors on Earth, but we don't know how.

We have two choices: (1) We can cocoon our families until Jesus comes, or (2) we can become re-creationists. One choice is based in fear. One is in faith.

Taking the faith route requires courage. I discovered this during the last few years as I have literally been thrown into the political and social arenas. I have had to personally experience the blatant intolerance of the pure message of Christ. In hundreds of media interviews, I have been put on the defensive as a representative of "unpopular" Christian views. Such topics as abortion, sexual promiscuity, homosexuality, pornography and traditional marriage are often viewed as divisive and extremely right wing. My prayer in these events is, "Lord, help me to deliver Your message in a manner consistent with Your character." Those opposed to my views have often acknowledged that I have not just come to debate, but to love. The apostle Paul warned us that in the last days, men would not endure sound doctrine. This is truly the depth to which we have fallen as a culture. The darkness of the hour has caused the spiritual vision of many to break down. Yet this has not always been the case.

Our forefathers saw the United States as a refuge from Europe's tyranny and as a country that could truly be governed by the principles in God's Word. The godly precepts espoused by our founders were too alluring to the rest of the world to be kept to one country. Thus we have seen the dream of democracy penetrate every continent.

Thankfully, God does not just dream of nations, cultures or societies. He is simultaneously passionate about the destiny of every person on the planet. God's dream also includes generations. He envisions a godly group of young people penetrating every realm of society around the world. In order to touch a generation, God needs an army of leaders. The leaders must be sharpened and prepared by one of the Lord's most strategic institutions—a godly family.

But who coaches the coach? Who trains the family trainers? Who better to tell us what to do to spread the dream of God than Ron Luce? I have known Ron for over a decade. I marvel at his wisdom in soul winning, his strength in discipleship, and his grasp of cultural trends.

This book is not just for parents; it is for the Church to read and learn what is needed to save our world. Ron shares statistics and stories that will convict any open heart of our great corporate lethargy to our situation. As a father of three children who have passed through their adolescent years dreaming the dreams of God, he is very qualified to serve as our guide.

We must find the motivation from the Holy Spirit to make a difference. Ron has led the way, and his principles have created the Teen Mania, Acquire the Fire and BattleCry events, and the many other missions of his organization. What about you? Where has God already placed you? Is it within the nest of your family home? Is it in your neighborhood, where you see teens who need care and direction? Wherever you are, you can—you are expected to—make a difference for God. Reach out, ask God for a dream, and take the information in this book with you. Get ready for the journey of a lifetime as you *ReCreate* your life, your world and your generation.

Bishop Harry Jackson
Senior Pastor, Hope Christian Church
Author, *The Warrior's Heart*

IT'S TIME TO RISE UP!

After exchanging pleasantries with some friends I have known since high school, I asked, "How's your daughter Bethany [not her real name] doing?" Immediately tears began to brim in both of their eyes as they described the latest in the series of events in their daughter's life.

My friends have been good church-going parents for all of their daughter's life. They are moral people and make a pretty good living. They have done seemingly all the right things to make them decent parents. But now, they recount how one minute after Bethany turned 18, she went out and got a tattoo. They tell me about how she lives at home but sometimes doesn't come home for days, and they have no idea where she has been. These despairing parents now await a few words from me that might bring hope in the most desperate situation in which they have ever found themselves.

The words in this book are for them and for all of the other parents just like them who need hope and help as they seek to raise their kids. This book is for the millions of parents who want to know what to do with their kids while they are still young in order to prevent a similar heartbreak from happening in their lives.

It's no secret that teens are in trouble today. Hardly a week goes by in which we don't see headlines about teens destroying their or others' lives. We see the effects of perverse rock and hip-hop music, but we don't know what to do. We know that Hollywood and MTV have a grip on our kids, but we have no idea how to protect them. Even good God-fearing parents are seeing their children affected by this culture of destruction.

Research now shows that up to 88 percent of kids raised in church do not continue in church once they enter college.[1] With statistics like this, the level of helplessness careens out of control in many parents.

So how can the average parent compete with the multibillion-dollar industries of pop music, television and the Internet all wooing the hearts and minds of their kids? Too many parents throw their hands up in the air and just "pray and hope for the best," because they feel that there is nothing else they can do. But right now, as you hold this book, hope rests in your hands.

Make no mistake about it; the pull of culture is strong. It manipulates our children at a young age into doing things that they would never dream about doing in their right minds. But the good news is that there is much we can do to protect our kids from the power of the culture that is destroying them. Our job as parents is not just to fight the culture but also to teach our kids to see through its shallowness and the motives of those who shape it. Our real defense is to build a culture in our family that is so strong and defining that *it pulls the hearts of our kids toward us* and keeps them looking to us to shape their values.

How many parents have I heard tell me, "But I have done all that I know how to do"? Therein lies the problem: *Maybe we do not know all that we can do!* The culture in which our kids are growing up is like no other in history. We cannot do the business-as-usual parenting that we've seen all our lives—not with a culture determined to destroy our kids.

The stories and principles that you are about to encounter are not just theories. This is a handbook of practical tools that have worked with our own teens, and countless other parents have found success because these are principles extracted straight from the manual for life: the Bible.

Our kids today are different from any other generation in history. They are more marketing savvy, media savvy, and culture savvy than any other generation before them. If we are going to build a strong culture in our homes for our kids and rescue them from a culture bent on deception, we have to start by recreating ourselves. That is why this book is different than any other you have ever owned. It's a book that you not only can read but also experience with friends. It's a book that is similar to how our kids experience things today. With this book comes a vast array of free parenting materials and stories found online to help you truly harness what you read.

Every chapter is accompanied by an online experience that goes along with the written words. That experience is found on www.battle cry.com. In fact, the full introduction to this book isn't even on paper; it's only found online. So go ahead. Put these printed words down for a few minutes and log on to watch the video introduction. The book will be here when you're done watching. (If you really want to experience how your kids function and multi-task, you could watch the video introduction online, while starting to read the first chapter and, at the same time, instant message a friend about this book and ask them to experience it with you.)

You may also want to get the workbook and video curriculum that accompany this book to go through with your spouse or small group. There are many action steps that will help you create the culture we are talking about so that you can recreate the culture your kids are living in.

Get ready for hope to flood your heart as you read these pages. If you have teens in the middle of teenage issues, you have come to the right place. The practical application contained here will also help you shape even your youngest children with *your* values. The days of helpless parenting are over. It is time to rise up and refuse to let this culture destroy our kids by creating a culture in our homes that is truly *irresistible*.

SECTION I

RECREATING THE CULTURE IN YOUR FAMILY

This book is *not only* for parents of teenagers. What you are about to read is written to convince you that it is imperative that you start actively working with your children at the very youngest age to create a family culture that builds stability, sets expectations and ensures security in their hearts. As your children grow into teenagers, you want them to have a strong foundation so that you're not struggling to pull them out of the pit of hell to barely survive with your family intact.

My wife, Katie, and I started the groundwork of keeping the culture from claiming our kids' hearts when they were very young—pre-kindergarten. We worked to build a healthy foundation for our family so that we could preclude many of the challenges we witnessed other people experiencing with their teenagers. After all, traveling every weekend, year after year, and seeing other people's teens hurting and broken, we knew what we *didn't want* our kids to become. So take a look around you and be aware of this culture that can totally wreck a young life as you seek to be parents who protect your children.

GENERATION OUT OF CONTROL

It doesn't take long to recognize that the forces of culture have sunk deeply into a moral abyss that resembles a horror film reeling before our eyes. Consider these headlines of news stories in the past year:

- 12-Year-Old Beats Toddler to Death with Bat, Police Say[1]
- Teacher Arrested After Offering Good Grades for Oral Sex[2]
- Pregnant High School Students in Denver Ask for Maternity Leave[3]
- Colorado Teens Accused of Killing 7-Year-Old Girl with "Mortal Kombat" Game Moves[4]
- Teen Accused of Trying to Rape 62-year-old Woman[5]
- Sixth-Grade Teacher Gets 10 Years in Prison for Sex with 13-Year-Old Boy[6]
- Michigan Teen Shooter Stopped Taking Medication Before Killing[7]
- Nevada Suspect Arraigned in Case of Videotaped Rape of Girl, 3 YEARS OLD[8]
- U.S. Prosecutor Accused of Seeking Sex with Girl, 5[9]
- Texas Girl, 6, Found Hanged in Garage Was Sexually Abused[10]
- Michigan Mom Gets 12 to 22 Years for Sex "Contract" on Under-age Daughter[11]
- Man Gets 20 Years for Bizarre Internet Love Triangle Murder[12]
- Four College Students Shot Execution-Style in Newark, N.J.[13]
- Young Mother Charged After Her 10-Month-Old Boy Was Recorded Sipping Gin and Juice[14]

How could these things have happened in a land built on such remarkable virtue? What kind of commentary do these headlines say about us as a whole? What so many of our Christian forefathers bled and toiled for seems to have suddenly and seamlessly slipped from beneath us. What happened to the decent and wholesome society in which to raise our kids that was once called America? How in the world did we come to this? Let's look at one glaring example that epitomizes how our secular culture can lure and destroy a young life.

The Britney Factor

I suppose the only people who don't know who Britney Spears is would have to have lived in a cave for the past 10 years. The stories of her recent public meltdowns have hit every tabloid and news show in the land. Her life seems to be spiraling out of control, with one bad decision after another broadcast for the world to see, resulting in unbearable public humiliation.

She started out as a fresh 15-year-old sensation. After starring on Disney Channel as a child, she hit the big-time. She got her "big break" and began singing and dancing for the world. In reality, it was not just her big break but also the recording industry's break, as they are constantly on the lookout for new talent to exploit (I mean, promote). These executives need new "eye-candy" to appeal to new audiences; so much of their business is to answer the question, *Who can we discover and make big so that we can sell more stuff?* Once the industry has a star, they must keep selling albums and keep people interested in their star.

Without much guidance from her parents, innocent Britney began to sing about the fact that she's "not that innocent" while she was still a minor. Tighter and skimpier clothing ensued in the rampage of her videos and magazine appearances. Then there was the unforeseen lip-lock with Madonna on national TV during the MTV awards in 2003.[15] It seems the more she pushed toward the edge, the farther she needed to go for the next round of PR to be satisfied.

Her visibility continued to beguile crowds; all the while the industry (that is MTV, Viacom, record companies, clothes and makeup companies) was making more off her persona. They maintained a very vested interest in keeping her public and giving her hints that would keep her in the public eye.

Finally, in September 2007, she was a last-minute addition to the MTV awards show to debut her new album. She was originally supposed to appear with magician Chris Angel, but he pulled out when he realized this was not going to be good. On the occasions when she actually came to rehearsals, with martini in hand, she found it hard to practice her dance routine. It was blatantly obvious to everyone that she was not ready for a live TV appearance. Both her wardrobe and her music needed some serious work. Yet MTV refused to pull her appearance, even though it was evident that public humiliation awaited her.[16] They knew that killer ratings were in store for them, and that's all they cared about.

While millions of people have been entertained and seduced by Britney, the industry has made millions of dollars. And while millions of people have been appalled and enthralled by her humiliation, the industry has made millions of dollars more. This cycle is part of a machine that uses people for the sake of ratings, not caring what it does to them in the process. Britney is not the only one. Many other young stars are in the machine. Consider Lindsay Lohan, the Olsen twins and Macaulay Culkin.

There are other casualties of this culture machine. Fans of the stars occupy the other end of the spectrum—the machine needs stars, but they also need fans to buy the albums and go to the concerts. The industry's job is to sell, sell, sell. It doesn't care what it sells or to whom it sells, just as long as the money keeps coming in. The antics of humiliated, confused and unpredictable Britney Spears are a picture of what the pop culture machine is doing to many teens trapped in the vortex of its destructive agenda.

Amy Winehouse is a prime example of what the machine does to people. In 2008 her album *Back to Black*, featuring the hit song "Rehab," won five Grammy awards. Amy was unable to receive the award in person because she had been denied a visa to enter the United States due to her recent drug troubles.[17] Think of the message this is sending out. Winehouse, who was once reportedly seen wandering around in her nightgown strung out on drugs, and who was recently accused of assaulting someone, is the person the machine chooses to exalt.[18]

The pop culture machine "cares" for your teens the same way it cares for Britney. The machine devours them and then spits them out. Lives are destroyed within the machine, as well as influenced by the product of the machine. Then the machine rinses and repeats, looking for the next product to sell and the next person to buy it.

How the Machine Works

There are about 71 million young people who make up what is currently the largest generation in American history, an estimated 33 million of whom are actually teens now.[19] Their number is so great that most marketers perceive them as an untapped gold mine—if they can just "embezzle" their attention and then sell to them. Right now, teens spend about $150 billion a year[20] and influence about another $200 billion of their parents' spending.[21] This is huge, but nothing compared to the lifetime spending potential of these young consumers. Marketers have documented that 13 is the age that many decisions are made for life-long buying habits. It's called the *branding age*. So if the machine can get them to like a drink, a clothing line or a musician by the time they are 13, they will probably buy those brands for the rest of their life.

"Of course, it is not the marketing that is the problem," as I told Vicki Mabrey from ABC News *Nightline*. "People are going to sell stuff and others will buy. It is the marketing without a conscience, without caring what you sell to teens and how it shapes them that is the problem." Much of what is sold to teens (and to children) is media driven (whether it's video games, websites, music, TV or movies). When confronted, most makers of media are quick to excuse their culpability by pointing to the parents who are responsible for what their kids see. While this is indeed true (we will deal with it at greater length in a later chapter), their entire machine is unequivocally aimed at selling to kids. If they could *not* sell to them, they would be out of business. They would not even venture to create the product unless they were convinced they could capture a critical mass of the market share. Truly, their industry thrives on the fact that most parents are either irresponsible or completely ignorant as to what the media that is sold to their teens actually contains.

Some parts of this culture machine (that actually manufactures teen culture) are staggeringly massive. Take Viacom for example; they own Nickelodeon, Nick Jr., MTV, MTV2, VH1, Comedy Central, BET, Logo (the gay channel), as well as other media outlets. They have what they call a "cradle to grave" strategy. They start when our kids are very young, getting them enamored with pop icons as they are baby-sat by Nickelodeon. Soon, they graduate to Nick Jr. and MTV, and their appetite for music and their desire to emulate the clothes, the vogue and every gesture of the hottest star is kicked into full function mode. They are happy to keep people occupied through every era and epoch of their life, making money as they maneuver them through their entire life cycle.

PBS reported in their special "Merchants of Cool" a few years ago how MTV has developed a prototype of what they want the teens watching their network to become.[22] *Mooks* are what they call the boys. They found that the more crass humor they built into their programming, the more teenage boys would watch. So they intentionally built new programs like *Jackass* and hosts such as Tom Green that constantly parade the Mook lifestyle (irresponsible, perverted, apathetic, use of crude humor, disrespectful) into new programs and MTV movies. The more teens watch, the more they emulate. The more they emulate, the more they sit on their couch and are consumed with the very ideal they are becoming; all the while Viacom is making lots of money. They are producing a whole generation of Mooks who are glued to their couch and consuming massive doses of the media that is created to keep them on the couch.

Midriffs are what they label the girls. The message they're sending is, "Hey if you've got it, flaunt it, even though you are underage. Act like you're older than you really are." So they promote stars like Christina Aguilera, the Pussy Cat Dolls, and, of course, Britney, to be the poster children of all this. They show spring break programs of high school and college girls showing skin and getting drunk. Of course, they never expose the stories of girls who get raped, get a disease or end up pregnant. Our girls then stay glued to their favorite starlet and, of course, mimic her clothing and lifestyle; except our girls (unlike those on TV) are having to pay the consequences of the lifestyle.

Viacom boldly proclaims, "We don't advertise to this generation; we own this generation." And in many ways it does, all while making about $3.27 *billion* in profit from destroying our generation of young people in the U.S. and around the world.[23]

Is it any wonder that 16-year-old Jamie Lynn Spears (the younger sister of Britney), star of Nickelodeon's *Zoey 101,* has turned up pregnant? The machine has done to her what it has been doing to millions of other girls from all over the world. It's no surprise that *Nick Jr.* did not cancel the show. Then they would have to admit that what Jamie Lynn has done is a shameful thing. Thus, millions of preteens now have their 16-year-old pregnant icon looming before them as a role model.

This machine is hungry. It must be fed. It needs more stars to control and exploit (what they would call *giving them a "big break"*). Who is really getting the big break? They also need fans to sell to. In either case, they do not care about the ultimate effect their machine has on its victims. Who's next? Is it the sweet Miley Cyrus of *Hannah Montana* fame, who will be sexualized to keep interest piqued? Is it your kids who will be the next Mooks and Midriffs to be produced by this machine?

Take another glance at the headlines at the beginning of this chapter. Look at the crop of fruit generated from this culture-marketing machine. See what it has done and is doing to your young ones. Is the next generation, who will be running our nation, being morally mutilated right before our eyes?

This thing called the culture machine seems so incredibly massive. What can be done? Who can change MTV? What can curb their appetite for more money and stem the tide of destruction? What can we do as parents? How do we protect our kids? Can we protect them? What about the future of our nation? Will this culture machine drive this young generation into a moral cesspool that would cause our forefathers to cringe in their graves?

That is exactly why you have this book in your hands. On these pages you will unearth a wealth of good news that can help you protect your family and preserve an entire generation. What you are about to read, if applied, will keep the culture machine from devouring your children, and show you how your church can be a rescuing agent for teens in your community. You will discover practical answers and authentic stories of teenagers, families and churches that are literally *recreating* the culture.

ARE WE NOT DREAMERS?

And after this I will pour out my spirit on all flesh. Your sons and daughters
will prophecy and your old men will dream dreams.

JOEL 2:28

Dreamers own us. They always have. Throughout history, those who dream the most compelling dreams are the ones who earn the following of the masses. Whether the dreamer is a political candidate who sweeps the elections or a general who compels men to follow him, those who have cast their dream with a captivating air have claimed the hearts and lives of the general population.

98 Percent vs. 2 Percent

It has been said (although it would be impossible to document) that 98 percent of our population are followers of culture and 2 percent are the shapers of culture. You can tell a follower of culture when you hear phrases such as:

- Did you see the movie trailer? I can't wait till the movie comes out next week!
- Every Thursday night I can't miss my favorite TV program!
- I have only seen that team lose three games this season!
- I've got to have those pants!
- I have to get my hair done like that.

These types of comments are indicators of a life patterned around the culture. The culture has determined what is essential, and people manage their time and money accordingly. Many people are actually proud of the fact that they have seen every TV episode of *24* or *Lost*, or that they never miss adopting the newest fashion style, which only emphasizes the control the culture has on them.

The innovative—those who dare to dream—are the shapers of our culture. Those 2 percent are the songwriters, the movie script writers, the inventors, artists, lawmakers, lobbyists, judges, video editors, network owners, record company executives . . . I think you get the picture.

Who are some of those dreamers? How about Bill Gates? He dreams about software; and if you're typing on a PC (as I am, writing this chapter today), you are participating in his dream (while he makes money, of course). What about Steve Jobs of Apple? Do you own an iPod? Every time you turn it on you are a part of his dream. Every time you download a song or podcast on iTunes, you enlarge his dream! These are two dreamers who have shaped our culture, indeed, our everyday lives, in a very real way. Who else? What about Martin Luther King, Jr.? Who can forget his indelible words, "I have a dream . . ."? We as a society are the beneficiaries of his dream for equality among the races. He ignited a movement of morality that made us all better human beings. But where are the other dreamers who can make us better as a whole? Where are the dreamers who can dream a dream to help people, rather than just sell something to them? Our country was founded by such dreamers, so where have they all gone?

Where are the people of God in the 2 percent? *Can we not dream?* Can we not conceive ideas to touch, rescue and affect the masses? Why is it that today, most of the dreamers who control culture are dreaming dreams that benefit only themselves?

Whether it is lyricists carefully crafting words of how to shoot an enemy to solve a problem or take advantage of young girls sexually, or makers of certain video games that teach our kids to blow people away, these creators of culture have been successful in transferring the wrong values to our kids' hearts and minds.

Our kids did not ask for this garbage.

Think about it. Most of the things that shape our kids' in this culture were sold to them. First, the ads spawned a desire in them for the product. Had they never seen the ad or talked to a friend who saw the ad, they would have never known they *needed* what the ad sold. Then merchandisers made it very easy to access and obtain what was advertised, or easy for adults to obtain it for them. The culture machine is not just media, it is stuff—stuff to see, stuff to watch, stuff to go to, stuff to wear, stuff to give, stuff to drink, stuff that makes you pretty, stuff that makes you cool, stuff that makes you popular, stuff that makes you sexy, stuff that is fun to do, stuff that is adventurous, stuff that will live your life for you so you don't have to go anywhere or do anything. Our lives are filled with *stuff*.

The problem arises when this stuff actually hurts kids because they cannot decipher the lack of positive values in the stuff, or when they don't realize that they are getting addicted to stuff. Think about it, there is overwhelming evidence that violence in video games and TV shows makes people more violent, to which more than 1,000 studies can attest.[1] A recent study from the University of Michigan reports that "Children's repeated exposure to violent television and video games is the strongest predictor of violence in adulthood," above any socio-economic background or issues of abuse.[2] Yet these creative geniuses use their creativity to figure out how to make the blood splatter more realistic on the screen in order to sell more product. They know it harms young people, damaging them long-term into adulthood, but they make it anyway. I say they are terrorists. *Virtue terrorists*. They are giving our kids candy with poison in it and laughing all the way to the bank.

Consider sex in media. Its only use is to sell more stuff and get increased ratings (to sell more stuff). Soft-core porn and sexual references are constantly grazing the screen, whether during regular family hour (averaging 6.7 times per hour)[3] or on MTV (up to 3,000 times per week).[4] All of this is done to make money. They say the sexual content does not affect kids, but there are a number of studies that prove what you and I, people with common sense, have known for a long time: it does indeed affect them. In fact, the Rand Corporation says that kids exposed to sexual lyrics and media programming are two times as likely to get involved sexually as those who are not exposed to it. They are two times as likely to have sex as a teen, catch a disease or get pregnant.[5] Some of these teens who catch the wrong diseases will never be able to have children; some will live in pain for the rest of their lives; and some will even die of a sexually transmitted disease; while others will have children at a young age, likely raising them in a broken home, and all because someone wanted to make money. Can you see why I call them virtue terrorists? They are ripping any kind of moral virtue from our teens in the name of economic freedom.

They keep dreaming of new *stuff* to see if they can generate an appetite for it. They are stooping to more extreme levels of depravity, hoping to rise above the noise made by the scores of products sold to teens. Think of the filmmaker who depicted 12-year-old Dakota Fanning being raped in a movie titled *Hounddog*.[6] They made the movie (what does that say about her parents, who would allow her to do the movie?) then brought it to the Sundance Film Festival and tried to sell it to movie distributors. It got a lot of media attention, but thankfully, not one chose to distribute it yet. But what does it say about us as a society that they thought they might be able to market it here?

What the Dreamers Know

Why do you think that Bill Gates only allows his own children 45 minutes a day on the Web?[7] Do you suppose he's trying to keep them from becoming part of the 98 percent who follow culture? Do you think he perceives the addictive nature of entertainment on the Internet? Perhaps that is why he refuses to allow his kids to get sucked into what he made effortless for the masses to access. How about Steven Spielberg and Tom Cruise, who will not permit their children to watch more than one hour of TV each day?[8] What do they know about television that we don't? Are they making sure their kids do not become "culture zombies"? They, themselves, are not part of this 98 percent, and they don't want their kids to be a part of it.

When we think of the 2 percent who lead our culture, we are forced to ask ourselves, *Are we not dreamers?* Are the only people who can engage our children perverted, money-grabbing dirtbags? Can we not dream a different dream for our kids and for all children in our communities? Cannot the people who follow the Creator of the universe be more creative and compelling than those who have a creative gift but exercise it in a way that hurts people for the purpose of making millions of dollars? Why does it seem that only secular people are part of the 2 percent? Where are the people with godly, Christian morals who are dreaming and shaping this generation? *Are we not dreamers?* Can't we dream a dream for our kids and for the kind of homes we want to raise them in that is stronger than the destructive culture all around them?

Can we not dream dreams that will protect the hearts and lives of our young generation? *Are we not dreamers?* Can we not think broadly enough for the youth so that when they get involved in our church and youth ministry, they are so consumed and enveloped with a passionate culture of fervent Christianity that they fall out of love with the things of the world? *Are we not dreamers?*

Can we not have a voice in shaping the culture of the entire nation so that our values are winsome and compelling? Could dreams provoked by our values actually attract people to our values and to the One who shaped our values, that is, the Lord Himself? That is what this book is about: provoking us all to dream at a family level, at a church level and at a national level. Now is the time for a new generation of dreamers to arise and unite. It's our choice if we're going to be a part of the 98 percent or the 2 percent. *In what percent will you be?*

All those who dare to venture forward in an exciting journey of shaping the culture—both for our kids and for their whole generation—continue reading and prepare for the most stirring adventure of your life, because dreamers are the ones who spark revolution.

THE INSIDIOUS GRIP OF CULTURE

The Latin for "insidious" is translated "to lie in wait for." If we look carefully, we will begin to catch traces of an insidious *plan* in our culture that is designed to entrap and beguile. This plan is devised by an insidious *enemy,* whose nature is treacherous and deceitful. The plan is carried out in an inconspicuous manner, seemingly harmless, but actually having a significantly grave effect, like an undetected disease.

This plan lures our kids (and us) into its trap by taking us to higher levels of entertainment and adventure than we've ever known. Then it wraps its claws around our necks and chokes the life out of us. Too often, even "good Christian" homes have found that they have been invaded by an amoral culture of destruction. But too many have found out too late, after living through a nightmare of a family life that proved to be a living hell.

Even *good* families are losing their kids.

Our culture is rife with stories of young people who have exhibited destructive behavior, even those who were raised in "decent" families. This behavior is sometimes isolated to the individual; and other times, the behavior is life-threatening to others. In recent years, some of the greatest atrocities have been committed by teenagers. Often these atrocities are even more shocking when we consider the wholesome families that raised the young people involved. Somehow these kids did not grasp the values of their parents. Whether or not the parents tried to instill these principles into their kids, it is obvious that the values that belong to one generation are simply not being handed down to the next. Let's look at a few snapshots of what is happening in our youth culture.

Matthew Murray

On December 9, 2007, we watched in amazement the reports of yet another shooter attacking a church, injuring and even killing some of the members. This was only hours after the same shooter killed two staff at the local Youth With A Mission (YWAM) campus. The shooter, Matthew Murray, was raised in a Christian home. Both of his parents were active members of their church and avid followers of well-known Christian preachers. They nurtured both of their boys in a Christian home-school program until they were old enough to pursue their own path of life. One son chose to go to a Christian university, while Matthew chose to attend YWAM and then worked on staff with a YWAM youth program. On the outside, Matthew and his family seemed to have everything going for them. But Matthew's inner life was inhabited by turmoil and despair.

Because Matthew is no longer alive, no one can really know what was going on inside of him, but his journal postings indicate that he was indeed searching for truth in a murky pool of teachings—messages as diverse as those from the Christian church to lyrics by the "shock rock" musician Marilyn Manson to writings of the late British occultist Aleister Crowley. However, even before Matthew began listening to Marilyn Manson, there is some evidence that he was depressed and even suicidal at the age of 17. What happened? How does a young boy raised in a Christian home not only become suicidal, but eventually homicidal?[1]

Eric Harris and Dylan Klebold

In recent years, there have been many shootings in America, but none that have shocked or shaken the world like the 1999 massacre at Columbine High School, near Denver, Colorado. After murdering 12 students and a teacher, and wounding 23 others, Eric Harris and Dylan Klebold committed suicide and sealed the vault of their journey on this horrific day in history. However, upon examination of both boys' families, there is nothing out of the ordinary that would raise suspicion of a violent behavior in these children.

Eric's dad was enlisted in the Air Force, which required relocation, as any military family would have experienced. After he retired, they moved to Littleton, Colorado, where he worked for a company that makes military flight simulators. His wife worked for a local caterer. Eric's parents tried to impress their strong work ethic onto their kids and were always supportive of their sporting activities. His friends knew them as "good parents." It wasn't until Eric was in high school that his parents started to see any reason to be concerned about his behavior, which prompted them to take him to a psychiatrist.

A "picture-perfect" family is how their neighbors described Dylan's family. Both parents graduated from Ohio State University. His dad was a real-estate agent and his mom was an employment counselor. The family attended a Lutheran church, and the two Klebold brothers completed their confirmation classes in accordance with Lutheran tradition. They also observed many Jewish rituals at home because Dylan's mom had a strong Jewish heritage. Unfortunately, even with strong religious influence and supportive parents, Dylan still ended his life immersed in a world of violence and hatred.[2]

Jamie Lynn Spears

When she was only six weeks old, Jamie Lynn Spears began following big sister Britney around the entertainment world as Britney performed for an off-Broadway show entitled *Ruthless*. At the age of 10, Jamie Lynn continued in her sister's footsteps by appearing in a Clorox commercial, which spiraled into a whirlwind of television appearances and regular roles on sitcoms. Even before Jamie Lynn was born, her parents were always hardworking and supportive. They paid for Britney's singing, dancing and gymnastic lessons no matter how financially challenging it may have been. Jamie Lynn's father was a building contractor, her mother, a first-grade teacher, and they worked hard to keep their kids in private school along with their extracurricular activities. They gave Jamie Lynn the same amount of support that Britney had, which is what helped propel her into a prominent role on the TV sitcom *Zoey 101*. However, at 16, Jamie Lynn's career was cut short with the news of her pregnancy in December 2007. The father is a 19-year-old boy she met at church and had moved in with for a while before the pregnancy was announced. Although Jamie Lynn is a celebrity, her story is no different from those of many other teenage girls across the country—many who also come from *good* families.[3]

Ben Thompson

Pastors' kids sometimes get into more trouble than all the kids in the church combined. Ben Thompson definitely proved to be one of those kids. Even though his parents had been pastors for 30 years, Ben still managed to find himself in the middle of a gang war with the Crips, one of the most notorious gangs in North America. He became involved in drive-by shootings and was shot at on more than one occasion. Even though he escaped the gangster life, Ben continued to be involved in destructive activity. After opening his own line of clothing, he began promoting it at nightclubs in Southern California, where he got caught up in alcohol and drug abuse as well as sexual activity. He became addicted to Speed, was suicidal, and got a girl pregnant who eventually had a miscarriage. Although he turned to his parents and to God for help after hitting rock bottom, the question still remains: How did he get there in the first place?[4]

Looks like the world did more training of this teen than his parents.

A Common Link

One thing all of these tragic stories have in common is that the kids were raised in "good, church-going families." Whether these tragedies were helped by the influence of their peers or the pull of the media, each of them were somehow manipulated and inundated by influences around them. These influences shaped their values more than their parents and the Church. As you read this, you can probably think of some kids in your church who got into some horrific trouble or experienced some kind of tragedy. The point is that you can't always measure the effect culture has on a young person until it is too late. This influence can, however, sneak up and destroy lives. As parents and adults, we've got to be the ones who see the enemy coming. We've got to be the ones who outsmart culture and protect our kids from this entity in our homes and communities that has the potential to destroy their lives.

HOW WE LET THE CULTURE INTO OUR HOMES

A man knocks on your door. As soon as you answer, you recognize him from the posters around town. He has just escaped from the prison not too far from your house. He's a known thief and sexual predator of young girls. He asks if he can go into your teens' bedroom to hang out with them for a while. Of course you say, "No way!" so he asks if he can just come into your living room and hang out with your kids without you there for a while. You say, "Absolutely not!" So he finally just settles for hanging out with the whole family as you watch a litany of popular TV shows that night as you spend "family time" together.

If we would not let that man into the rooms of our kids (whether male or female), why would we let a TV or computer reside in our kids' bedrooms? These modern occupiers of time dispense a river of polluted entertainment riddled with the same values driving the visitor at your front door. Why would you let all those people into your house? In many cases, parents have done just that. Every time we let unsupervised media into our homes and into our kids' minds, we have invited a terrorist into our home. Let's examine how these terrorists plant their values within our precious children.

Video Games

Recent studies reveal the following statistics about computer games and video games:

- 79 percent of American children now play computer or video games on a regular basis.[1]
- 67 percent of homes with children have video game equipment.[2]
- Children play video games for an average of 8 hours a week.[3]
- Video game sales bring in $17.9 billion a year.[4]
- 80 percent of video games played by kids feature aggression or violence.[5]

Looking at this data alone, you can see an entryway for an insidious part of our culture to enter our homes. We think we're just buying games for our kids to play and keep them occupied, or maybe because they think it's cool and they "really want it and all their friends have it"; so we acquiesce and say, "Okay, you can have it too." Little do we know that what we're really doing is acquiescing to the world's values.

Computers

Think of all the websites and community sites like Facebook and My-Space. On MySpace alone, of 110 million users, approximately 13 million are between the ages of 12 and 17.[6] Facebook has more than 70 million active users, approximately 4 million of which are between the ages of 12 and 17.[7] Just think of the number of kids on those sites sharing their hearts with "friends" that parents have no idea about. Of course, we've all heard about online predators. A recent story on CBS News reported the following:

> As many as seven girls from Middletown, Conn., were assaulted by men they met on MySpace who lied about their ages, police said. The girls were between the ages of 12 and 16 and authorities said the men who touched or had sex with them falsely claimed to also be teenagers.

Two unsolved murder investigations also involve MySpace: the case of 15-year-old Kayla Reed, whose body was found in a canal near her Livermore, Calif., home; and the case of Judy Cajuste, a Haitian 14-year-old from Roselle, N.J.

Cajuste's body was found in a park dumpster, badly bloated and possibly disfigured, according to sources close to her family. Her body was assumed to be that of an adult, so Judy's single mother was not notified for more than a week.[8]

We read lots of stories of kids posing online in sexually explicit photos, like they see in magazines. In addition, they end up chatting with people they don't know for hours upon hours at a time. We have even heard some recent stories of kids who have committed suicide because of messages that have been left on their website.[9]

There are adults who go online for hours at a time, and there are virtual worlds for kids too. Some examples include Disney's Toontown Online, Nickelodeon's Nicktropolis, Club Penguin and Final Fantasy XI. Virtual worlds are simply online sites that let you pretend you are someone else while you pursue fake relationships with other people doing the same. It's hard to control. Are the kids making real friends on these sites or are they spending time with predators? What manner of values are they discovering? What kinds of conversation are they having? This is just another example of an entryway flung wide open to a negative part of today's culture.

Cell Phones

Cell phones are a huge avenue of communication for kids as well as a personal entryway for the worldwide media to connect with your teens. Much of the text messaging, or texting, that young people do, while seemingly innocent, can be a huge labyrinth of trouble. The conversations they have by way of texting, unsupervised, can lead to many exchanged words and concepts that would horrify you. In fact, many of the teacher predators we have heard about on the news began their relationship with younger students via texting.

- Parents often give cell phones to children as a safety precaution.
- Cell phones give predators secrecy and time to groom children for sex.
- Recent teacher-student sex abuse claims involve texting and cell phone use. Experts recommend limiting the features on kids' cell phones.

Consider this recent article about this very topic:

It's happened again. A teacher is accused of having sex with a student and, like many times before, cell phone calls and texting reportedly had a role in sexually abusing a minor.

The same cell phones that parents buy as safety devices for their children are the gadgets that pedophiles and predators use to prep kids for sexual encounters, experts and police say. . . .

The wooing via text messages, cell phone calls and e-mail is so subtle, so affirming and so indulgent, that by the time a teacher makes inquiries involving nudity, a child probably isn't alarmed, Ramsey said.

"They will be supportive of behavior that the parent would not be supportive of, and the child gets an opportunity to do things that they cannot do at home," Ramsey said. "That is like a teenage dream." . . .

By the time she started e-mailing porn and illicit messages, he trusted her. "She would ask me if I was a virgin," the boy is quoted by police as saying. And she starting asking him about his interest in knowing about oral sex, police notes state. . . .

"If you think your kids are protected because they know that if they are touched in their private areas or if somebody undresses in front of them or attempts to perform a sexual act that that is the only bad thing, then they are not going to be prepared for the subtle, the grooming piece," Thompson said.

And there's something else Thompson recommends. Limit a cell phone's abilities. Allow it to make and accept calls to and from parents and 911 only.

"I know the societal pressure is for parents to get their kids the latest phone with all the gadgets that are out there," Thompson said, "but more important than complying with all the societal pressures is protecting your child."[10]

Friends

It is imperative to know who your kids spend most of their time with. What kind of talk goes on at school? What's being said in the locker room? Who are their best friends? And in particular, what is going on at overnight parties and sleepovers, even when they are young? Are they staying with their friends the *whole* night?

Most parents don't imagine that they have any control over what are considered "normal" activities in their children's lives. How can parents control who their kids' friends are or what they do? How can parents possibly know what is being said or done when their kids stay the night at another person's house? These are all difficult questions, but they are not unanswerable.

We need to wake up to the fact that what seems to be the "normal way kids grow up" can actually pose entry points for the culture to begin to shape their minds and hearts.

Dumbed-down Reading

Many of the magazines aimed at teens are nothing more than propaganda promoting pop-culture icons and willy-nilly values that are passed down from the editor to the reader. *Seventeen, Teen People, Cosmo for Girls,* and a whole slew of music and pop magazines for guys keep them salivating for more of the culture. At first glance, we might think these are just fashion and glamour magazines, but they're actually imparting a huge dose of the culture that it would be best to inoculate your kids against.

For example, a recent *Seventeen* magazine issue came out with blatant pornography—photographs of female genitalia with all the Q&A that a girl ought to be asking her mom about in the privacy of her own home. Some of the questions were, "Would I have my period if I was pregnant? What is the best time for sex? Is it normal to think about sex a lot? Is it normal to have pimples near my vagina?" In another issue of *Seventeen*, the lead article was "How to Tell if You're a Lesbian"; the second article was "How to Tell Your Parents That You're a Lesbian"; and the third article was "How to Have Safe Lesbian Sex." At the very least, these kinds of magazines are occupying your teen's time with mind-numbing information on what this pop star's doing or that pop star's doing; at the most, they are proactively instilling the wrong values into our kids.

In December 2007, Sean Hannity invited my daughter Charity and me to appear on his program to debate Julia Allison. Ms. Allison is the editor-at-large for *Star* magazine, just one of many publications in America that promote the values we continually see destroying our precious daughters. Sean asked me to discuss the impact that sexual content in ads, magazines and movies has on young people. He then wanted me to debate Ms. Allison, as she is a firm proponent of teenage sexual rights.

Ms. Allison acutely stated that we "seriously can't expect young people to not have sex." The way she communicated her bias was not subtle whatsoever—from her viewpoint, there was absolutely nothing wrong with teens being involved sexually. To her, the notion that any parent could keep his or her kids away from having sex is absurd and ridiculous. The horrific reality is that this same person is writing the articles that most of our daughters of America are digesting every week.

Music, TV, Movies

Everything I've already mentioned is under the umbrella of entertainment. But in particular, entertainment in the form of movies, television and music is what is shaping our young generation. Although we consider them entertainment, they are actually *infotainment*. They impart values and information about the world, maybe information about life, that your kids are not ready to process and absorb.

The problem is that too many parents use these avenues to keep their kids occupied and to witness just a part of the "unavoidable" culture in which we live. Television, for example, broadcasts some 20,000 sex scenes that the average young person will view by the time he or she graduates from high school![11]

Take a look at some of these stats:

- Movies have an 87 percent likelihood of presenting sexual material.
- More than 3 out of 4 Americans say that the way television programs show sex encourages irresponsible sexual behavior.
- 64 percent of all shows include sexual content, and only 15 percent mention abstinence, protection and consequences.
- 59 percent of parents say their 4- to 6 year-old boys imitate aggressive behavior from television.

- 60 percent of parents say they are "very" concerned about the amount of sex their children are exposed to on television.
- Among shows with sexual content, 5 scenes are shown per hour overall, 5.9 scenes are shown in prime time per hour, 6.7 scenes are shown in teen shows per hour.
- 83 percent of kids, 8 to 18, have at least 1 video game player in their home; 31 percent have 3 or more video game players; and 49 percent have video game players in their bedrooms.
- More than 80 percent of children live in homes that have cable or satellite TV service.
- American children, ages 2 to 17, watch television on average almost 25 hours per week, or 3 hours per day. Almost 1 in 5 watch more than 44 hours of TV each week.
- On average, young people spend almost 4 hours a day watching TV and videos.[12]

The point is, every time your children watch any one of these things, not only are they absorbing the values of the creators—the dreamers—of these products, but the content of these products is also numbing their own ability to dream.

Dream-Killers

If we are to be a part of the 2 percent of dreamers that shape the world, and if we are to raise kids that are part of the 2 percent, we've got to make sure they don't get absorbed into the 98 percent. Not only must *we* be the dreamers, but we must also teach our kids to be the dreamers for their own generation. Note this passage of Scripture: "Your young men will see visions" (Joel 2:28). Our young people need to have a vision of how God could use them to change their generation and make a difference in the world.

Every time they watch, listen and participate for one hour, two hours, three hours, four hours to a website, a movie, a magazine, their hearts are being taken in by someone else's dream, if only for that short time, and these teens stop creating culture for themselves. The fact is, *we must either be the dreamers, or we will be a part of somebody else's dream.* Every time we allow our kids to watch, see, feel, touch and embrace this culture, they become a part of a dream belonging to someone else. Every movie, every song, every website and every magazine was, at one time, someone's dream. When we pay admission to go see a movie, for those two hours, we are a part of the filmmaker's dream. As we allow our kids to be immersed in the culture, they become so charmed and engrossed in the vast ocean of others' dreams that it robs them of the aptitude to dream their own dreams.

Our job is not only to protect them from the maelstrom of a negative and harmful culture, but also to inspire them to be the ones who dream. We should not be people who blindly parade into combat against everything about the culture in hopes of changing something. It won't work. But we can and must create a *new culture* in our family that actually transcends the pop culture so that our kids can clearly discern the difference and be wise enough to avoid being lured in.

We must be careful what we invite into our living room in the name of entertainment. If you let the wrong things in, these terrorists will seduce your kids, impart harmful values and, in doing so, inject poison into your kids' worldview that could follow them for the rest of their lives. If we can perceive the perils of a depraved culture all around us, surely we are smart enough not to invite a terrorist into our living room.

A CULTURAL DASHBOARD FOR YOUR FAMILY

It's easy to discuss the idea of what other people are doing. You're not really a part of that; you're not really shaped by the culture of the world. Oh, yeah? All of us have the potential of being deceived and shaped by what we see and hear. It's easy to think, "Well, Ron, you're talking about all of those *other* families who don't really care." I'm sure that the parents in chapter 3 said the same thing. So I'm going to give you some practical insights in this chapter to help you see how much the culture might be affecting your family. This is something to keep visually in front of you to see whether or not the culture has begun to overpower your life and that of your family.

How Many TVs Do You Have?

Some parents think it is a sign of blessing their kids to give them what they never had when growing up. A personal media device that feeds a child day and night in his or her bedroom—I have even heard of a ministry leader who allows his son to watch movies with his girlfriend, in his bedroom, on the bed, with the door closed—is *not* a blessing. Katie and I could have afforded to put a TV in each of our kids' rooms, or given them stereos at a very young age, or filled their lives with video games. But we didn't want to give them easy access to media and risk their addiction to it. On our family TV set, when our kids were small we got about three scratchy channels. Sure we could have afforded a dish or cable, but we didn't want the world invading our home and taking our kids hostage. I think much of the conveniences that many people now consider a necessity are more of a curse than a blessing. Moreover, we need to be careful about justifying getting that cable *for the kids* when in reality, we're talking about the sports and movies that *we* like, and *we* would have to sacrifice if we decided to shut it off.

Do you have rules about what your kids can watch? When our kids did watch TV, they were very compliant about what kind of shows they could watch. We tried to teach them *why*, even when they were small, they should not watch certain things. For example, we did not allow cartoons with witchcraft in them, or programs that disrespected parents. We explained how this was just the trick of the Enemy to make all things that go counter to the Bible appear really attractive. We trusted our kids to be discerning, and there were many times when they would initiate turning the channel when something harmful hit the screen—with no need for us to say anything. Still, it is impossible to predict when a lewd commercial is going to come on, or when a crass sexual joke will slip across on a TV program.

Do you have rules about how much TV your kids watch each day? At the height of our kids' TV viewing, they were watching an hour a day max, and maybe two hours of Saturday morning cartoons. Yes, they did watch various other children's videos and movies, but that is more of a controlled substance.

How Many iPods or Other MP3 Players Does Your Family Own?

Do you know what songs are on your kids' iPods? Is there an approval process in your home for acquiring music? Have you taught your children proper music listening etiquette? From the beginning, our kids knew, when they first got CD players, that they could never have headphones on while in the car or when other people were around. We wanted them to realize that this "personal music device" was not going to dominate their lives or ours. We wouldn't let listening to music substitute for family conversations.

Just because your children may want a music device such as an iPod or an MP3 player doesn't mean that they should have it. As the parent, you need to choose when these things are appropriate and realize the implications they bring. These are not just cool devices that enable them to listen to music but also an invitation for music to be a full-time part of their life. In giving such devices to your children, you are basically allowing it to be something that can dominate their lives.

Think about this in regard to any type of media. It might be that computer or video game devices are taking up all of their time. Don't get sucked into the idea that because you're giving them cool gifts you're a great parent. Instead, realize that these "cool" things are actually forms of media that can begin to form a wall between you and them, influencing them more than you do.

Whenever you do feel the time is right to give these types of devices to your children (as I mentioned, my kids didn't get an MP3 player until they were 16), the gift should always come with conditions. These can be:

- You can only listen to it for [x] hours a day.
- You can only listen to music I approve of.
- You are not allowed to have your ear buds in while in the car, because in the car we are talking to each other.

Also, talk with your kids about listening etiquette so that they do not get the attitude that because they now have these devices, they can pour music into their brains 24/7. As a parent, you can create conditions with some built-in freedoms, but you're still shaping their lives and the culture of your home.

How Many Computers Are in Your Home?

I hope you have guidelines regarding how much time per day your child is permitted to be online or playing computer games. Our kids have always had the "one hour per day" rule. For some of you, your kids would go through massive media withdrawal to do this because media has been way too involved in occupying their time.

Is there a computer in your kids' bedrooms? I hope you have surmised by now that you would NEVER want to allow this to happen. This is dangerous territory. Our one family computer has always remained in the front room area, where we can easily monitor who is online for how long (some screening software like Net-Nanny can do that for you). As soon as my oldest daughter graduated from high school, we bought her a Macbook (which is really not a computer at all, but a traveling media-go-anywhere machine). We told her she could do homework and other projects OFFLINE in her room, but anytime she was online, she needed to be in a public area of the house.

Do you know what sites your children have visited? Is this invasion of privacy? Yes, and it is your right as a parent. You set the guidelines upfront on how the computer is to be used, and you also will want to know all the places/people/friends they are involved with. That is your job as a parent. This way, there are no surprises when you look at histories of where they have been on the Web.

Do you have Internet protection software on every computer? It's not that you don't trust your kid; it's that you don't trust the world. Studies show that *9 out of 10 kids who regularly do homework on the Internet get an unwanted sexual message online.*[1] Parents, we must be smart. One time, I was sitting in shock before a room full of ministry and family advocate leaders as a Department of Justice official asked us how many of us had protection software on our computers. Only 3 people and myself in a group of about 60 raised our hands! How can we complain about the world when we don't do what we can to protect our kids?

Media on Cell Phones

Getting your kids a cell phone is not just a communication device from you to them. It opens up a whole world of communication with peers in ways that you may never know about, and a whole world of media they are exposed to and can access at any time.

Have you enabled text on their phone? You can get them a phone without texting abilities (or you can disable it). If you do that, they will think they are in the Stone Age, because all their friends have it, but it could protect them from aimless conversations, especially with "friends" you do not know. Plus, it will protect them from running up exorbitant text bills into the hundreds and even thousands of dollars. Recently, the *Washington Post* reported a story of Sofia Rubenstein, 17, who recently sent 6,807 text messages in one month alone.[2]

If and when you decide to turn on the texting abilities of your child's cell phone, let him or her know that there are limits to how much texting they can do, when they can do it, to whom they can do it (only people you know), and that you would be looking at their texting habits and conversations on a regular basis. *No freedoms are ever given without responsibility and accountability.* Make sure to limit or prohibit photo texting. You can prohibit sending photos with your carrier to keep your kids from being a part of possible photo-passing frenzies.

Consider some of these excerpts from recent articles on this very topic:

Cell Phone Porn Scandal Hits U.S. School

ALLENTOWN, Pa.—Police faced a difficult if not impossible task Thursday as they tried to stop the spread of pornographic video and photos of two high school girls, images that were transmitted by cell phone to dozens of the girls' classmates and then to the wider world . . .

At least 40 Parkland High School students believed to have received the images would not face prosecution as long as they show their phones to police by Tuesday to ensure the images have been erased. But students at the school said the distribution was far more widespread . . .[3]

Cops: High School Students Traded Nude Pics of Themselves Over Cell Phones

FARMINGTON, Utah—Police are questioning a group of teenagers accused of trading nude pictures over cell phones.

Farmington Police . . . say six or so Farmington Junior High School students took pictures of themselves and then shared the naked images.

A parent of one of the kids found the pictures on their child's cell phone and called police. Detectives say the 13- and 14-year-old boys and girls questioned said they took the pictures as a joke, but it's potentially a crime . . .[4]

Trading Nude Photos Via Mobile Phone Now Part of Teen Dating, Experts Say

COLUMBUS, Ohio—Forget about passing notes in study hall; some teens are now using their cell phones to flirt and send nude pictures of themselves.

The instant text, picture and video messages have become part of some teens' courtship behavior, police and school officials said.

The messages often spread quickly and sometimes find their way to public websites.

"I've seen everything from your basic striptease to sexual acts being performed," said Reynoldsburg police Detective Brian Marvin, a member of the FBI Cyber Crime Task Force of Central Ohio. "You name it, they will do it at their home under this perceived anonymity."[5]

Is the Internet disabled on your child's phone? This can prevent your child from getting unwanted messages and videos from the Web. In England, much of the revenue acquired from cell phones is generated from porn downloaded onto them, and it is rapidly coming our way. This will prevent them from surfing when you are not around and keep them from "buying things" on the Web, like songs and ring tones that you don't know about (and then are billed for later in the monthly statement).

Information on Limiting Cell Phone Options

AT&T Phones

Smart Limits can be installed for a monthly fee that limit the following:

- Number of text and instant messages
- Dollar amount for downloadable purchases (ring tones, games and more)
- Times of day the phone can be used for messaging, browsing and outbound calling
- Who the phone can call or text (incoming and outgoing) by blocking and allowing certain numbers
- Access to content inappropriate for children

MEdia™ Net Parental Controls

MEdia™ Net parental controls are included at no additional charge with most wireless services. With a compatible handset, these controls will:

- easily restrict wireless access to mobile websites, as well as restrict purchase of premium content or subscriptions
- restrict access to sites with mature content inappropriate for children (content filters)
- prevent children from buying premium content (such as ring tones, games and graphics) that is direct-billed to the account holder (purchase blocker)
- turn off a specific service for the month once a limit is reached
- enable you to program allowed numbers (such as your own and 911) that the phone will always be able to call even if the limit has been used for the month (there will be a notification the action is restricted and the service will be stopped until the next billing cycle begins)[6]

Verizon Wireless

Verizon Wireless allows parents to check how many minutes their kids have used any time during a billing cycle. Parents can choose to block all text messages.[7]

Video Games

The same rules as I've already indicated apply. When playing video games, are your kids in the front room (not the bedroom)? Do you have a restricted amount of time per day policy? Are you aware of the content of every game so that there is no "teaching to kill" or shooting of human beings practiced?

Checking the Culture Invasion of Your Home

Lest you think we are only addressing issues that affect "less responsible" parents than you, ask yourself these questions and see how you score:

- How many quotes from movie dialogue have you heard out of your mouth or your kid's mouth in the past 6 months? (Or in the last week?)
- How many quotes from ads have you said or heard your kids say?
- How many times have you heard, "But Johnny does it" or "Johnny's parents let him do it"?
- What happens when all of your family is gathered around a TV program and someone interrupts to get something or accidentally flips the channel? How violent is the response? Does everyone get mad? Do they yell real loud, "Shut up!"? It may be an indicator that you're so into the media that you value it more than the actual people in the room with you.
- Do you find yourself acquiescing to your kids' requests just to get them off your back so that you can have peace in the house? You let them watch that movie; you let them have that video game; you let them have that magazine; you let them wear those questionable clothes.
- When is the last time you bought something you didn't really want to buy for your kid after she saw so many ads that she just *had to have it*?
- Can your kids quote countless lyrics from their favorite pop songs, but not much Scripture?
- What would your kids say if someone asked them, "What are your TV rules?" or "What are the Internet rules in your house?" or "How are the rules enforced and how are they implemented?"
- Do your kids know what is happening with Jamie Lynn Spears (younger sister of Britney Spears) right now, but they have no idea what your family values are?
- Do they always forget that they have a church activity on a certain night, but never, ever forget what night their favorite TV show airs?

- Do they know the storyline of multiple TV shows but have no idea of your family heritage?

If any of these touched a somewhat sensitive spot or hot button regarding your family, then perhaps it may be true that you've had more invasion of popular culture than you were aware of. The good news is that *it doesn't have to stay like this*. You can turn your family around and proactively shape the hearts and minds of your children. Not only can you do that, but you *must*. It is the only hope your children have in the midst of a culture that is bombarding them with missiles of deadly assault at a velocity once unthinkable but now a bitter reality.

CONVENIENT PARENTING = BRAINWASHED KIDS

"But they can't help it! They were born that way, and I don't think there is anything wrong with the gay lifestyle," says your 15-year-old son. You are aghast; you can't believe what you're hearing from your own child after being raised in your home. A Christian home!

"Mom, I think I'm in love with this guy who is 17, and I want to know about protection because I think I'm ready for sex," says your 13-year-old daughter.

"Your son has been expelled from school for beating up another young man," the junior high principal tells you.

"I really feel like this book I'm reading makes a lot of sense to me and is true. So I'm not going with you to church anymore; it is just for old-fashioned, fake Christians," says your 16-year-old *enlightened* daughter.

"Who says abortion is really wrong? I think a woman ought to have a choice with her own body," your 18-year-old says, as she's telling you she's just discovered she's pregnant.

"But I didn't raise you like that!" you exclaim. "I raised you better than that!"

Did you really? Did you raise her at all . . . or did the media? How is it possible that kids can grow up in the very homes of people who say they love Jesus and believe the Bible, but have such different values? *Somehow we have allowed the media to kidnap and brainwash our kids while they sit in our own living room! We have allowed terrorists into our homes!*

Where else did they learn that . . .

- Gay people are born that way?
- Giving your purity away before you are married is even an option?
- Beating up a peer is the way to handle a disagreement?
- If they feel it, it must be true?
- Abortion is an issue of a woman's choice, and the precious baby alive since conception has no power to negate that kind of decision?

Despite all of our best intentions as parents, too many of us have adopted the TV and other technologies as a convenient distraction, and even as baby-sitters, for our kids. Starting at a very young age, we have set them up in front of a TV program, a video or a video game so that we can "get things done." Or we regularly appease a child who whines until he gets his way to watch a movie that you know has less than godly values. While it seems harmless enough, you will discover in a brutally shocking revelation, like one of the conversations listed, that it is indeed harmful. And by the time this conversation takes place, it may be too late to reverse.

Parents simply cannot entrust their kids into the hands of those whose values are warped and unchecked in the name of entertainment. They must not grant the makers of media free access to their young people anymore. In case you haven't yet noticed, we as a society have leapt off the ledge of moral common sense. The days of mindlessly allowing our kids to be transfixed with the media of their choice are over if we hope to raise this generation with any kind of real moral conscience and wholesome living.

How Did It Happen?

Most families are two-income families (approximately 80 percent of married couples in the United States are now dual-income earners, meaning that both the husband and wife work outside the home to provide a solid, consistent income for their family[1]). If we were to glance into an average home with young children, we would probably peer through the window at a cyclone of activity. The parents (or parent) get the kids up and ready and to school, come home from a full day at work, rush off to after-work activities, feed and bathe the kids, as well as maintain personal hobbies. It seems like we run out of time real quick, doesn't it? After all, the dinner's on the stove and someone's calling on the phone . . . so what's the kid to do? It's true that a lot of parents work hard to get their kids to after-school activities to help them build their social relationships. But it's no longer the way that you and I grew up, when to occupy our time, we would go outside and play, either by ourselves, with our siblings or with little Johnny down the street. Now the path of least resistance is having something electronic absorb the dull moments, in whatever form that might be.

We've grown into a nation that constantly wants to be tantalized. Our kids have grown up in a society where one still moment lacking excitement among a constant stream of entertainment equals immense boredom. From a parent's point of view, allowing the children continuous entertainment also engages a parent's selfishness, because we don't want to hear the kids complaining or whining. For our own comfort, we say, "I'm being a good parent. Why not get him the next video game? Why not let him watch this video again? Why not let him watch Nickelodeon, or whatever?" So it really is a *parenting of convenience*. We can assuage our guilt to our heart's content by saying, "The other kids are doing it"; "It's the new way of parenting"; "Oh, there are some good morals and stories on this network." But the fact is, the kids are being enticed into a brotherhood of media and technology rather than establishing connections with real people.

Dad is busy with his career. Mom has her career as well, or she's busy being a mother with a million details to manage with a handful of kids and all their activities. You tried to get them on a sports team, but they just didn't seem to assimilate into sports. There are no kids in the neighborhood for them to easily play with. So one afternoon TV show leads to the next, and then the trend continues on into the evening. One video game drifts into another (*Oh, look how they are playing with each other* . . .) as a friend comes over to play video games with your son. Are they really playing *together*? One website "for kids" leads to another.

Before you know it, they have logged more hours on media than they have spent with you each day or each week—even more hours than they have spent at school by the time they are 18. If your teen attends all 180 days of school, at 7 hours a day they average 75,600 minutes in school, 224,640 minutes with some sort of media, and a mere 2,002 minutes talking seriously with their parents in one year. The average parent spends 3.5 minutes in meaningful conversation with his or her kid each week compared to 72 hours of media per week.[2]

Who do you think will have more influence?

Parenting Is Sacrifice

Parenting was never supposed to be easy. No one ever called it simple, effortless or painless. If you ever put your kids on remote control because you have all sorts of "electronic baby-sitters" available to occupy their time, you can say that it really doesn't affect your kids, but if they're still in the process of growing up, how can you be sure? The bottom line: *parenting equals sacrifice.*

"But I don't have time," a parent may say. "I have so many pressures at work; I am trying to provide for my family." It's a seemingly rational explanation, but the question is: *Provide your family what?* More of the stuff that the media machine is trying to sell? Wouldn't you rather provide a safe, loving environment to impart your values to your kids?

It's undeniable that as a parent, you *will* sacrifice *something*. You can choose to sacrifice up front: time, sleep, career, hobbies while your kids are small. But I guarantee that you will also reap joy and delight as they grow up. You will gain a lifetime of intimately knowing them and the privilege of helping them grow into seasoned, productive, godly adults. *If you don't sacrifice up front, you will sacrifice later.* Think about scenarios such as your child getting pregnant (or getting someone pregnant) as a young person, multiple times. Imagine living through your child's divorce (perhaps several times) and playing the visiting game with divorced in-laws for the rest of your life. Can you picture a 35-year-old old couch potato camping out on your futon because he can't hold down a job?

Your kids will be old a lot longer than they are young. I know people in the older generation who have had grown kids cause them misery and regret for *their entire adult life*. Boy, now *that* is a sacrifice. Even if you do it for purely selfish reasons, sacrificing up front to spend the needed time with your kids in order to raise them well will protect from life-long sacrifice.

Dream for Your Kids

You can protect your kids from the disaster of being shaped by a confused generation of adults selling media, but it will take deliberation. It will take sweat. It will require emotional and mental engagement with your kids, starting when they are at a very young age.

You're the only one who can do it. You are the only one who can be your child's mom or dad. There are masses of other people who would love to entertain them; there are plenty others who would be glad to take your money for occupying your children's time and keeping their voices from whining. But *you* are the only person who can deposit your values into them. You're the one who has the opportunity to take them on hikes and walks and campouts. You're the only one who can have long talks about your family history and about what the future holds. Lots of other people can take care of them. Lots of other people can give them food and change their diapers. But you are the only mommy and daddy they will ever have.

So my encouragement for you now as a parent is this: *Dream a dream for your kids.* What kind of child do you want to see standing before you when he or she is 14 or 15? What kind of young person do you hope for when he or she is 17 or 18? Are you planning to have, or do you already have, a house filled with spoiled couch-potato mooks wanting everything handed to them as if they're entitled to it? I'm sure that's not at the top of your wish list. Most parents with kids like that did not plan it. They just did nothing to prevent it. They let the media appease the whimpering of their children while small and continued the routine through their teens. Do nothing and you will get what MTV and others have intended for your kids: a fresh, hot batch of mooks and midriffs.

It's time to dream a dream for what they could be. What do you want your kids to be like when they're 21 or 22? Do you want them to save their virginity for marriage? Do you want them to be pure in heart and mind? Do you want them to be responsible human beings who serve their community? Do you want them to be active in their church? Do you want them to make an eternal contribution to the kingdom of God and the lives of people around the world?

Basically, do you want them to be entertainment oriented or service-to-others oriented? Ask for an entertainment-oriented person, and you'll get someone who is constantly appeasing the flesh and desiring *the next thing* to engage and tantalize them. Where are the servant-oriented people—those men and women who lay down their lives as a sacrifice for others? It is our choice as parents to determine what kind of young people we want and what it will take to produce them. If you dream a dream and roll up your sleeves and go for it, I'm confident that you will raise the kind of child you will be proud of for many years. If you sacrifice *now*, you'll reap a blessing *for the rest of your life;* and the world will never be the same.

You can navigate through these dangerous waters of popular culture, but you are going to have to learn how to captain the boat. What you are about to read and, I hope, digest and apply will protect your kids from the destructive part of culture and show you how to effectively plant your values in them.

Merely giving birth does not make you a parent. Sacrificing while your children are small, laying down your "deserved" freedoms and deeply thinking about how you're shaping your children will ensure their lifelong freedom from the chains of slavery to our culture. It's work, and it's called loving your children. It's called being a parent.

WHO OWNS THEIR HEART?

When your kids are very young, it's easy to see that you still own their hearts. They look up to you with an adoring gaze, wanting to please you—partly because they don't want to be punished, and partly because they literally idolize you and believe that you can do no wrong. At that point in your child's life, he or she has not seen many of your flaws yet. As your child starts to get a little older, however, her gaze of adoration begins to wane. Many times, between the ages of 6 and 8, you'll hear your child say things such as, "I want that toy I saw on TV," or "Mommy, why can't I play with . . . ?" or "Johnny gets to do it, so why don't I get to do it?" All are telltale signs that friends have begun to own your child's heart a little more than you do.

The change in ownership is not something that happens dramatically. However, there are subtle signs that friends are beginning to hold more authority than you do. Your children begin to respond to the cues they get from their friends about what to wear or what to do, to a greater degree than the cues you give them on the same subjects. They develop a frame of mind that cares more about pleasing their friends than pleasing you. This thought pattern begins in very small ways, but each small thing you see is a sign that your child's heart is being lured away from you.

Some people would say, "These little things are all just part of growing up." And it's true that most parents don't worry about it. Yet the questions their children ask, based on feelings of peer pressure about why their friends get to do so and so and they don't get to do so and so, are met with responses like, "Because I'm not Johnny's parent, am I?" "Just do what I say" or "We don't do that in our home." While these responses are partially true, there is a deeper issue here: Is it really a "natural part of growing up" for our children's hearts to be given over more to their friends than to their parents? I'm not so sure. It may be a familiar part of growing up, but it doesn't mean that we can't stem the tide of the transference of their affections. It doesn't mean that we're doomed to lose our children, or that there's sure to be incessant fighting with the "because I say so!" kind of mentality from now until the time they leave home.

The small changes that signal a pulling away continue as we start to see the "boy crazy" or "girl crazy" years between the ages of 12 and 17. That's when we tend to hear things like, "I've got to have that CD; it's just coming out"; "I've got to wear these clothes because they're the coolest thing ever"; "I've got to watch this TV program"; "I want my MTV!" That last telltale statement of defiance shows the formation of the attitude, "I want the culture that's shaping me to continue to shape me, and I want to embrace it." Many times, too many parents have acquiesced just to get their kids off their back and silence the relentless complaints. They justify this acquiescence by saying, "It's really not that bad. It's just music television, for crying out loud, right?" "It's just some new clothes" or "Yeah, it shows a little bit more skin than the clothes that we wore when we were young, but it's just part of the culture."

All of these signs—that the culture owns more of our children's hearts than we do—start when they're young. What that ultimately means is that the culture has more impact on our children than we do. The culture defines them, owns them and possesses them. After all, when MTV says, "We don't advertise to this generation, we own this generation," in many ways, it's really true.[1] What they say goes. What they put on their network sells. We can say, "As long as you're a part of my house you're not going to watch that" or "You're not going to wear that," but such parental responses don't really get to the issue of who owns a child's heart.

Somewhere in the process of this heart defection—moving from the influence of parents to the influence of peers and the culture—kids are turned into machines that don't want to hear anything their parents have to say. They don't want to talk over things with their parents. They don't want to accept their parents' instruction. If they do, they do it begrudgingly and with the wrong heart attitude. They're not willing to embrace the values we're trying to get them to embrace.

Heart defection may be a "natural" part of growing up, but it's not inevitable if we as parents jump between our young ones and the culture that's out to claim them. Whoever owns their heart will have the most influence on them.

The Heart Meter

Parents, you are the ones to intervene in your children's lives to keep them from being pulled away by the culture. To do this, you need to develop a "heart meter" for your kids by watching for the signs—even when they are very young. Watch who owns your kids' heart and mind, in each stage of growth, and who they get validation from. When you start to see signs that your kids care about their friends or what the culture thinks more than what you think, it should be an indicator for you to "lean into them more." When I say this, I don't mean that you should point your finger at them and say, "This is the way it's going to be." You have to lean into them *relationally*. You need to woo their hearts back from the culture or their friends so that you are their touchstone. You are the one they go to for advice and direction. But it takes constant monitoring of who owns your child's heart. You can tell this early on by little statements they make.

As our girls were growing up, my wife and I could see these signs show up even sometimes in relation to the kids in children's church or the kids down the street who played with them. Whenever our girls made a comment such as, "Well, she gets to do . . ." we would try to jump in the middle of that. When I say "jump in the middle," I mean that we became aware of a red flag that somebody or some force had invaded the hearts of our children, and we needed to intervene quickly. The way we did that was by investing *time*. We jumped in and began to spend time with them, talking about the issues they might be bringing up and why our values were different from what they would like to do. I'm not talking about giving one lecture after another and hoping that something would stick, but talking and spending time so that an affinity was established through a heart-to-heart connection, resulting in their caring more about what we thought, allowing for more opportunity to impart the values that were most important to us.

It's sort of like the jockey riding a horse. As he rounds the corner, he leans a certain way. He watches cautiously. That's what parenting is—watching our kids for the signs of who owns their heart and making the necessary course corrections. Watch for little indicators—phrases or slogans they use, quotes or songs from movies or from advertisements. Then start looking at where the signs are coming from and see if they're spending too much time with the wrong friend or with the wrong media. You're already curbing their media intake, as a good parent will, but even so, never go on autopilot.

When kids say things like, "I don't care what you say," and we say back, "You'd better care, because this is the way it's going to be in my house," we might succeed in controlling their behavior while they're in the house, in that moment, but we're not going to succeed in wooing their heart when they're not around us 24/7. What are they listening to when they're at school? How are they dressing when they're at school? The world is rife with kids who dress a certain way at home, but as soon as they get to school, they peel off a layer of clothing to dress as suggestively as they'd like to. Are they being obedient according to the letter of the law or according to the spirit of the law when you're laying down guidelines for behavior?

When it comes to matters of the heart, *you can't command the heart; you've got to woo it.* It's our job as parents to woo the hearts of our kids so that they *want* to listen to us. If we allow the culture or their friends to overpower them, it becomes incredibly difficult to regain their respect, but it can be done.

Wooing Your Child's Heart

When my girls were growing up, even when they were only one year old, I would spend time with them by taking one or the other of them with me when I traveled on weekends to events for teenagers in arenas around the country. We did fun things. For example, when I had a break, we would sneak out in the middle of a busy preaching itinerary to go to an amusement park or to a children's museum. When they got a bit older, we would go to a concert in the town where I was speaking, or go out to a nice dinner.

Through their teen years, I would regularly "date" my girls. When I saw signs of their pulling away or that their hearts were not fully engaged, I would "lean back in" and say, "Hey, let's go grab some coffee" or "I'm going to get up early and take you to school so that we can grab breakfast or coffee on the way and talk." What that meant, literally, was that *I got up earlier*, by a couple of hours, in order to make room for that time together. It took sacrifice, but it's called being a parent. I've also done the same thing with my son. We look for new adventures where we can bond and build memories that begin to draw his heart toward me.

Whether the adventure is a late-night coffee, even when I don't feel like it because I'm tired and I know I've got to get up early; or whether it's a late-night 2- or 3-mile run with my daughter Charity at the end of a busy day (when I've preached my guts out at a Monday night service and just got home at 11:30 P.M.), part of wooing my kids' hearts means spending that time together. I call this time "leaning in."

Leaning in means finding creative, relational ways to spend time together so that you're not just sitting in a room, with nothing else to say but "Hi, how are you?" *Leaning in hard* requires that you spend *lots* of time together doing fun things. Your initial conversations with your child might be a little bit awkward. You want them to share their heart; you want to get close to them, but their attitude and non-response may be shouting, "I don't want to talk to you. I don't want to be with you. What are you doing this for?" Just remember that this is part of your job as a parent. If you've found that your kids don't really talk and share their heart with you, well, all the more need to lean in. Don't try to probe and provoke them to talk to you right away; just be there doing stupid and fun things with them. Eventually, they will talk. And they really do want to talk; they just want to make sure that you're the one they want to talk to.

Men, start doing things with your sons. Make a "date" (or a "bud-grub," as some call it) each week or every other week to go out to breakfast or just do something that they like to do, even if you don't like it. You could do paintball or some other kind of adventure sport, or go see some monster trucks or something else where they're not expected to talk all the time. Why not do something way out like make dinner for the women of the family? You'll have a great time of laughter and bonding, and you'll thrill Mom!

When you lean in hard, your kids will soon get the message that "Wow, Dad cares about me; he wants to listen to me." It may not happen during the first week or the first month. It may not even happen after the first three or four months. But if you keep doing it, what's going to happen naturally is that they're going to open up; they're going to start sharing their heart.

If you're tired of asking, "How are you doing?" and hearing, "I don't know"; or asking, "What do you want to do?" and hearing "I don't know," just keep leaning in. I know it can be discouraging. But don't give up. Even though those answers are a kid's standard response, to indicate that he or she is not interested in sharing much with you, do not give up. You can't force intimacy, but you can woo it successfully. Depending on how hardened your kids are, or how controlled and manipulated by the culture and by their friends, it might take you some significant investment of time to win their hearts back; but it's not impossible.

Remember, it's our job as parents to *woo* our children's hearts, to *keep* their hearts and then to *influence* their hearts. When that happens, they will become the God-honoring people we've always dreamed they would be.

WINDOWS TO THE HEART

"My kid just won't talk! Every time I ask him a question, he just gives me the same answer: 'I dunno'!"

Does conversation with your teenager sound like that? If so, let me share with you an idea that my wife and I learned when our kids were very young. It's called *Windows to the Heart*, and it's a very simple concept. A "window to the heart" means that there are moments that arise every so often that contain a peculiar vulnerability to engage your child's heart and mind. You can recognize these candid moments in a question or see it in a glance.

When your kids say something that demonstrates *openness*, pay close attention. Openness might come through a question such as, "Mom, do you think I'm pretty?" or "Dad, what do you think I'm good at?" Or it may be a comment like, "I don't think anybody likes me," or any number of statements that linger, awaiting your response. Rather than automatically responding, "Of course you're beautiful," or "Of course people like you," recognize that a window to your child's heart is wide open, and your perception of those window moments can lead to significant life discussions with your child.

The trouble is, you can never quite predict when a window to your child's soul is going to show. It could occur at any waking moment. Most of the time a window is opened at an inconvenient moment when we least anticipate it. We need to be constantly on the lookout for such a moment of openness and, without hesitation, *leap through the window*.

Don't give in to the passing thought, "Oh, honey, let's just talk about this in the morning." Seize the moment!

At times, the window might sound like, "Mom, can we talk?" or "Dad, I want to share something with you." But most times, your child may just start sharing something with you about his day, and you might feel like saying, "Let's talk about it tomorrow," or "I'm too tired." The fact is, the window is open now, and you don't know if it will be open tomorrow. Of course, as parents, we're thinking, *Why wouldn't it be open tomorrow? Tomorrow's as good a day as today, and I would be more alert if I could get some good sleep. I'll be able to think and pray about the answers I want to give.* None of that makes sense to a kid who's hurting and just wants to be heard. You might come back the next day and say, "Hey, let's talk about that thing . . ." and your child will respond with, "Oh, no, I'm fine." Now the window that was open yesterday is shut tight. You can try to pry it loose all you want, but it will not open. And you can't force it.

How to Encourage an Open Window

The window to your child's heart has a much higher probability of opening after you do some activity together that has nothing to do with a serious topic. For example, when you play a nonsensical game or go somewhere fun where your child feels an atmosphere of love and trust and affection from you, the window will probably begin to squeak open by the end of the night, after your time together. Yes, you're tired. You would have been happy for the conversation to come up earlier, maybe over dinner or coffee, or during one of the activities you were doing. But no, your child wants to bring up a topic *now*. The prudent parent will see the crack in the window and take the cue. And even though tired, he or she will ramp up again to go through the window, because open windows are few and far between.

So when your kids invite you to do something with them, even if you don't feel comfortable, and may not want to, the fact that you *do it* and *do it with them*, even when it makes you look stupid, sends a message to them. It bonds you to them and proves that they can trust you with their hearts.

One time at the beach, one of my kids said, "Come on, Pop, let's go dive into the waves together." I had already jumped in, and now I wanted to relax. I wanted to read, but there was an opportunity for a shared experience with her. "The water feels amazing; you've got to jump in these waves," she said. And so I did. I took the cue and responded to the fact that she was waiting for my presence. The same is true of your children. When they want you to do something with them, even when you would prefer not to, *do it anyway,* and your child will connect with you on a deeper level and will be more prone to openness with you.

Inconvenient Times

Windows to the heart usually open at times when you don't want them to. Most often, late at night. Of course, sometimes kids are being manipulative in order to stay up later—they just don't want to go to bed yet. But there may be a lot of other times that they're very sincere and really do need to talk. The fact is, even if your child is being manipulative, it may still be an opportunity for an open exchange. So what if they go to bed a little bit later? How much more valuable is the fact that you connected heart to heart with your teenager. You can't always tell if your child is being sincere, but always give your child the benefit of the doubt. Once that window is open, jump through! Statistics show that people who have ended their life tried to talk about it with someone first.[1] So either no one listened or no one took them seriously.

The number of late-night conversations I've had with my girls is incalculable. Usually it happens after I've had a hard day of work and they've had a hard day at school. I peek in their room late at night and see that they're awake when they shouldn't be. I could give you a number of examples when this has happened, like two days ago, with my daughter Charity. I was exhausted after a long day, and she said, "Hey, you want to make me a cup of coffee?" I said, "You want one?" and she said, "Yeah, let's have one together." That was a cue that she wanted to spend time with me; she wanted to talk. I was really tired; I didn't want to talk. I just wanted to go to bed. But I value the openness of my daughter's heart more than my own sleep. I would be able to sleep later; the window of her heart might not ever open in the same way again. If I didn't carve out that time with her, it might have created a memory that whispered, *When I'm open, he doesn't want to talk to me.* And I'm not going to let that thought happen between us.

The window to your child's heart will likely open while you're busy with work, or while you're watching a movie, or while you're on the Internet, or when you're really engaged in something other than talking with your child. But as parents, we need to be responsive to the cues that our children want our presence, even when we're throwing ourselves into something else and we're insanely busy. Those signals of an open heart could be unfolding all around you, all the time, and they are *way more important* to attend to than being entertained with a movie; *way more important* than watching a TV show or reading a book or answering emails.

The Deepest Part of Your Child's Heart

A teenager is going to talk to *somebody* about what's going on in his or her heart. The question is, Will it be you? If it's not you, will it be someone with far less wisdom? Will he or she go to a peer? Studies show that most kids join gangs because they're looking for the closeness of family that they don't get at home.[2]

Your kid's heart will be vulnerable to those who are listening to him or her. Is she sharing her heart online on MySpace? It's tragic when a kid blogs his or her pain for all the world to see because Mom and Dad, sitting 10 yards away from where the child sits typing away, are too busy to listen. If you haven't had a heart-to-heart talk with your kids in a while, you need to find out who they're sharing their heart with. But do it in a very subtle way. Start creating opportunities to show tangible love so that perhaps the window to their heart will be opened to you once again.

Remember when I said that parenting requires sacrifice? Every time you have a late-night conversation with your teenager, you are sending a positive message, and a window to his or her heart starts to creak open. Your tangible interest and love are what draw your child's heart toward your own. That's what you want above all else. Because whoever your children open up to are the ones who will have the most influence on shaping their heart and life.

COMMUNICATING YOUR VALUES

"I didn't raise you like that!" an exasperated parent says after finding out his kid got drunk for the first time. "How could you do this?" a parent wails, when finding out that her child has had homosexual contact, or has had sex, or is pregnant. My question for the parent is, "How *did* you raise your child?" Or did the media raise your child? Who is having more effect on your kids, you or the culture? It's easy to believe that you do, but you must not take it for granted. You must be proactive about how you communicate your values to your kids, and do it in a clear way that engages them. After all, the culture is very proactive and aggressive in the way it communicates its values!

Think about this. G-rated movies make way more money than PG, PG-13, or R-rated movies.[1] Although many G-rated movies have some questionable values, most of them are wholesome and family oriented. So, why are not all movies G-rated? If they are the best moneymakers, why wouldn't Hollywood throw all of its energy into making the most amount of money possible? It's because there is an agenda. There are values that the movers and shakers of this culture are trying to communicate. The machine would rather sacrifice the money so that it can impart its values. If the voices that hold sway in our culture are so proactively imparting values of destructiveness and violence and sexualization, shouldn't we at least be just as strongly proactive about imparting our own values?!

A Code to Live By

What are your core values? It's easy to say, "I just want my family to follow the Bible," or simply quote the fruit of the Spirit (see Gal. 5:22-23). Often, we find that when we say we just want to follow the whole Bible, or a preset list of qualities, we end up practicing *none of them*. We end up emphasizing none of them. It's more effective to create a list of about three to five values upon which to build your family name, heritage and practices. What are the actions and attitudes that you want reflected in everything you do? What do you want the foundation of your family to be?

Identifying your list of core values requires that you and your spouse think through the question, What kind of kids do we want to raise? If nothing else, what are the four or five characteristics that you would like to roll off the tongue when people think of your family? More than anything else, what do you want to instill in your kids and see them identify as their code of values?

Katie and I created our list when our kids were very young. We came up with many qualities, or values, and realized the list was too long. The Bible talks about how a good name is hard to find; it's more valuable than silver or gold.[2] Based on that proverb, we asked ourselves, "What do we want our lives and our family reputation to stand for?" We reduced the list to four values and backed up each value with a passage of Scripture that best embodied each idea.

It's a common practice in the business world for a business, in order to shape its culture, to establish *core values* and then rally every employee around those values. Doing this begins to actually change the culture of the workplace. You can't just change the culture because you want to; you must get people to accept and support the values that you are suggesting.

I began to wonder if the same concept might work in my family. So we decided to establish some values. We didn't just say, "These are our values." We got the family to really shape their lives around them. After doing all the work in advance, and thinking through what our four values would be, and selecting the Scriptures that best represented who we wanted to be, we decided to make the family core values a great unveiling.

We made it a big event for our family—a defining moment. Cameron was about three, and our daughters, Hannah and Charity, were only eight and nine years old. We told them, "A week from today, we are having a big family celebration. It's going to be something exciting that we've never done before." When we said that, they shouted, "What is it? What is it?" And we replied, "Sorry, we can't tell you any more. It's going to be a big surprise." Each day we would tease them a little bit more. "It's going to be so great. We are all going to get dressed up!" They would say, "Really? Can you tell us what it is?" Then we'd say, "Sorry, we can't tell you more. It's going to be on Friday night, and it's going to be great! We're going to have a special meal. Oh, sorry, we can't tell you any more . . ." We built up great anticipation in the kids.

When the big night arrived, we all got dressed up and had a big meal together. Katie and I cooked something really fancy that we knew the kids would like. Then we had a large mysterious *something* set up in the living room, covered with a tablecloth. We lit lots of candles to add to the vibe. After the nice dinner, we brought everyone into the living room. We said, "We care about our family name, and we care about all of us going in the same direction together. It's important. *A good name is hard to find; its more valuable that silver or gold.* We care about the character of our family." I took a brick and a hammer and—SLAM—broke the brick in front of them. I said, "See this brick? It's not strong in itself. What's inside the brick is what makes it strong. It is what's inside our family that makes us strong— and what's inside is our character. Tonight, we're talking about what will make us a strong family so that we can build something strong together. Mom and I have been thinking and praying about what we, as a family, want to stand for. So we want to show you our four core values . . ." And with a grand *swoosh,* we unveiled the masterpiece.

We had the core values written in calligraphy on parchment paper so that it would look similar to the United States Constitution. As you can see on the next page, it reads "Character of the Luce Family."

We listed the core values and then explained to our children what each meant: *honor, respect, honesty* and *responsibility.* We had the kids read

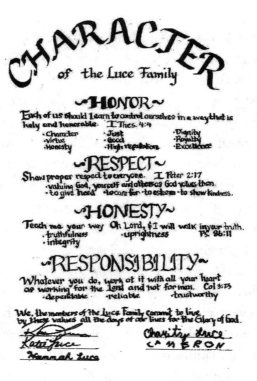

each of the Scriptures that went with each value and had *them* answer what they thought it meant to live each value. "Do you think this is a good foundation for our family?" we asked them. "Do you have any other thoughts or comments?" They shared some of their ideas.

We then said, "If we are all in agreement, then we want to make a covenant together that *this* is the kind of family we are going to be. It doesn't mean that we are going to be perfect; but this is what we will constantly strive to show each other and other people." We each signed the parchment. Then we prayed together and sealed the moment. We have our family covenant framed and hanging in our house right now. We made copies to put in our kids' rooms and had it placed on things like mugs and shirts to make the core values visible every day and easy to remember. (By the way, I had a video camera set up in the corner of the room, so we captured the family meeting on film.)

How to Use Your Core Values

Core values need to be reiterated over and over. A one-time ceremony is great, but you need to talk about the values every time you confront a child about a rule or when you need to discipline your child. During those times, you say, "The reason we have this rule in our house is because it relates to this core value." Katie and I were constantly relating life to our core values as we talked with the kids. Every time we disciplined our children, we explained, "This core value is why I don't want you to lie, and this is why we are disciplining you. If we don't have honesty between each other, we don't have any trust in our family." When we disciplined, we might say something like, "These are your core values too; did we not agree on this?"

In order to make core values meaningful, you have to be able to confront each other in the family on any violation of the contract. This is an area that some parents do not want to hear about! There will be times when we, as parents, violate a core value. When we do, we either need to be quick to confess it to our kids or to acquiesce if they confront us about it, and say, "You're right, please forgive me." *It's very important that you do not act as if you are perfect.* If you want your kids to respond in a positive way to the family core values when you confront them about it, then you need to model the values. Regarding the core values, everyone is at the same level in terms of confronting each other. Sure there is a hierarchy in a family, with the husband and father as the head, and the wife in authority over the children. But when it comes to the core values, the children can say, in a very respectful way, "Mom, Dad, that was not very honest . . ."

As parents, we cannot be so arrogant as to never admit when we are wrong. It's very important to explain this to your children as you initiate the core values so that *everyone* is responsible to not just practice them but to confront anyone who digresses. Teach your children to respectfully confront you if they see you violate the core value. It's very important for us to do everything we can to *live the values* ourselves—not just in front of our kids, but all the time. This becomes the foundation for family trust and confidence. It's who you are.

Core values are the strongest, and have been internalized when the children talk about them and confront each other about living them, even when you are not there. You know that your children have adopted the values as their own when you hear them say to each other things like, "That is not very honorable" or "We don't watch that kind of stuff."

Your family core values ought to answer "why" to every rule you have and every action you take. Instead of saying, "Just do as I say," tell your children *why*—because what you are asking your children to do or not to do is one of their core values that has been taken straight from the Word of God.

Echoes from Others

It's important for there to be other people in your kids' lives that uphold the same kind of values so that their words and actions become "echoes" of your own. When your kids see the values lived out in the lives of other people—aunts or uncles, people who are significantly younger than you, or young married couples the kids think are cool—they will be strengthened to live the same way. No matter how good your parenting is, your kids get tired of hearing only from you. But when there are other people around your kids who have the same values, they become an echo to your values. They say it in a way that will strike a different chord. It will resonate in a different way. Your kids will feel validated, and they'll know that other families live the same way.

Covenant Friends

When Katie and I were very young parents, some incredibly wise parents told us that the biggest mistake they ever made was to let their kids stay overnight with other kids. That seemed to be where all the trouble started for their kids, who were now teenagers who had gotten into quite a bit of it. There is a strange kind of peer pressure created, and an inordinate amount of influence on your children, when they are engaging in an all-nighter with someone else's kids, and you have no idea what that family's values are.

We made a decision when our kids were small that they could not spend the night at any friend's house. We modified that rule a little to say that they could stay the night at the houses of *covenant friends*. Covenant friends are parents with whom we have a relationship and know that they are raising their kids with the same values we have. We know that their kids are going to have the same kind of morals instilled in them. We know that the parents are going to be supervising our kids as well as their own.

Sometimes our rule about sleepovers meant that the girls could not stay the night with a friend down the street or even with their cousins. This is where it gets a little sticky, because we don't want to offend our relatives. However, one horrible conversation could destroy a whole bunch of work you are trying to do in the lives of your kids. If your children are only 8, 9, 10, 11, imagine if they had an exchange of thoughts and conversations with other kids, where rebellion is deposited, or something is shared about sex, or your kids are exposed to some movie where swear words are prevalent or it contains concepts that you just don't want in your kids' minds. Children are just too young to understand, not to mention the possibility of their sneaking out from a parent's supervision. We have stuck with this rule through all the years that our children were young, and I encourage you to do the same.

Talking About Your Values Regarding Media

Katie and I made it a habit that whenever we saw something on TV, or in a movie, or in life that directly violated our values, we would talk it over with the kids. Even though our preference was for them to never see it, there are some things you just can't help seeing, whether it's the Victoria's Secret posters all over the mall or an ad that flashes up on screen. We had countless conversations with our kids in the car that started with the statement, "What was the story you got out of that movie? What do you think that movie said that doesn't agree with the Bible? What do you think was their real message?" I would do this after going to Broadway plays, which we have taken them to over the years. We would always ask what they saw or heard that contrasted with our family values system and the Bible's teaching.

When we would see a show about a person falling in love, we would say, "What about that love story? We know it was sweet and interesting, but what about it didn't agree with what the Bible says about love? We know that the Bible does not say anything about 'falling in love.' Love is a decision you make to commit yourself and serve someone and sacrifice your selfish tendencies. You may have felt infatuated, but those feelings do not mean it's real love, right? That is the lust of Hollywood's invention." The kids would say, "Yeah, totally."

If you want a fighting chance of instilling moral fiber in your young people, it is going to take some thought. They will not accidentally pick it up without a word from you. So instead of your kids being a blank chalkboard for the world to write its values on, fill them with truth and help them buy in to the values from the Bible that will give them the best chance for a great life. Please note: Just because your kids say they believe in Jesus, and they go to church, does not automatically mean they have assumed all the values and lifestyle of the Bible. It is our job as parents (not the job of the pastor or youth pastor) to compel our kids to see the virtue of our core values and help them adopt them as their own.

A MESSAGE IN A MEMORY

A great portion of family culture is built on folklore—a collection of narratives and memories, some true, some false; some funny, some harsh. But they make us who we are and create an atmosphere in our family that defines us. One of the keys to proactively crafting a family culture is to constantly be thinking, "What kind of memory am I creating right now, whether good or bad?" It's not just, "What am I doing right now for my family?" or "How much am I earning for my family?" or "What am I giving my family?" But "What kind of memory am I etching into the template of my children's minds?"

Many of us have suffered from the illusion that simply earning extra money to give our family more stuff is what will help them. Often we end up substituting material gifts for the time-intensive process of creating meaningful memories. And often we forego the effort of creating memories that would cost near to nothing but would create great family tales and significant ethical lessons for our children to store in their memory for the time when they create their own family heritage for their own children.

Bad Memories

Everyone carries some bad memories from childhood or more recent events. Bitter or hurtful memories can become part of the foundation on which children reflect for the rest of their life. The question is, How have we, as parents, played a part in instances that might linger in our children's minds and contribute to shattering a tender childhood?

At the very least, have we unwittingly created an atmosphere of distrust in our children toward us? There is one overarching principle to bear in mind when it comes to sheltering your children from bad memories.

When your children do something to make you angry (inevitably they will, because they are young and will make lots of mistakes), be careful how you react. A parent's reaction to a child's actions is the bulk of what stays in the child's memory. If you erupt in fiery anger, the *last thing* your child will remember is what he or she did, the meaning of the words you shouted or how they *should have* reacted. Children will, however, remember that livid look on your face, the harsh tone of your words or the humiliation they felt.

Some parents even resort to swearing at their kids and belittling them, making them feel like worthless idiots. Unfortunately, some kids' whole lives are filled with one bad memory after another. They can recall very little of the positive things that their parents said or the treasure of exciting experiences they had. It's important that when we as parents make a mistake, we go in and do everything that we can to make it right by asking forgiveness. That's right—I said parents need to ask their kids to forgive them. Many kids have never heard a parent ask their forgiveness. Even if you really blow it and make a big mistake, you can turn the whole memory around based on the heartfelt sincerity of your apology. (Of course, I'm not using this as a license to make huge mistakes on purpose.)

I can recall an instance on one of our family vacations when my girls were 13 and 14 years old, and my son was 7. We were on a cruise ship, and the girls rushed back to the room later than when they said they would be back. Even though they were only 10 minutes late, I made a big deal and was very angry about it. My anger was motivated by the fact that I was terribly alarmed. They were on a cruise ship and were supposed to be with friends; but they could have been anywhere. I was about to start a panic search all over the boat. My fear for their safety was unleashed in anger.

Afterward, I realized the damper I had put on the vacation experience. I had not truly communicated the intentions of my heart and the reason why I had responded so angrily. I knew I was in danger of leaving them with a memory of this entire vacation as *the night Papa got mad and wrecked our vacation.* Dramatic action was required.

When the family got up the next day, they weren't sure whether I would still be mad. I had gotten up earlier and met with God and felt the rebuke of the Holy Spirit in my heart, and began to ponder what I could do to make it right. Once everyone was up, I asked them to forgive me. I told them it was unnecessary to be so angry. Although what they did was wrong, my reaction was also wrong. I asked them if we could start the vacation over. They said okay. I said, "I want you to forget about last night. I'm going to walk out the door. When I come back in, I'm going to tell you what I was really feeling in my heart last night."

When I walked back in, I began to tell the girls how worried I was about them and how precious they were to me. I wouldn't want anything to happen to them. With tears streaming down my face, I got on my knees and began to hug them, saying, "I'm so thankful that you are safe. Please don't do that to me again!"

Needless to say, they forgave me. There was opportunity to build something positive on the lingering negative memory. When we talk about that vacation now, the anger incident never comes up. There is definitely a way to redeem a negative interaction with your children if you remember that you are not just living your life, but you are also creating memories that will replay inside of hearts and minds forever and ever.

Good Memories

One of the things that constantly run through my mind as a parent is a tally of what good memories I have created this year, this month, this week for my kids. Those memories are the hard drive from which they will recall their lives.

As I said in an earlier chapter, from the time my kids were one year old, they started traveling with me. I travel and speak almost every weekend during the school year, doing events called *Acquire the Fire* at some location with thousands of young people in an arena. I always took one of them with me as soon as they turned one.

In between my preaching and ministry times, I would find something to do or somewhere to hang out that was *all about them,* so that they wouldn't feel like they were just tagging along.

Here are a few of those memories, some small, some not so small. But I always tried to be aware of and proactively set them up. During my ministry trips away from home, we would:

- Sneak away at lunch time to go to an amusement park that was close by.
- Go to a child's museum where they could do crafts
- Go play miniature golf if we got there early enough on Friday before the event.
- Have late-night dessert when we got back after an evening event.
- Order room service.
- Take a walk on the street late at night. When we were in a city like Nashville, we would walk the street and listen to the bands play, grabbing a milkshake or cup of coffee along the way.

At-home memories:

- Late-night Jacuzzi talks. One of the few things we have wanted since the kids were very young is a hot tub. With our intense schedule, it has been a good place to relax. It has also served as a good place to have family time as we talk and laugh and just sit together.

- Katie read novels to the kids. She home-schooled our kids until they were in junior high or high school. They have their memory banks full of sitting on Mom's lap, listening to story after story of the classics as well as the books they were going through with the home-school curriculum.

- We always made a big deal of putting the girls to bed when they were young. When I was home, I would put them to bed by reading *Aesop's Fables* (or whatever they requested) and praying over them. Somewhere along the line, the girls decided to put together what they called "a parade for Papa" before the reading would begin. When I walked in the room, each night there would be a different array of blankets on the floor arranged with dolls and animals. As I opened the door, there were my two little princesses doing ballet, calisthenics, gymnastics and flips for me. Then they would grab me by the arm and I would usher both of them up the "walkway" they built for me and sit on the "throne" they made out of pillows with each of them snuggled up by my side as we read stories and prayed until they drifted into slumber.

- During most of their time growing up, we did a *family night* every week. Each family member got to choose an activity on their week, whether it was watching a movie, eating out or playing a game. Our challenge was to find something creative and "outside the box" that would not just be a fun activity, but would also create a great memory. When we remember our family dates, "crazy hair night" was a big one where we all did another family member's hair in a really wild way and then went out to dinner. We did a pajamas night and a '50s night and all kinds of other different things. It's not a bad idea to get your kids to help in choosing what these memories are going to be.

In some of the memories you make, your kids are a little bit more elaborate than you. Remember, it's important, especially when they are small, to not just go where you want to go. Go to a place that will be a great memory for them and be a great family time. Some vacations are more "let's all relax and do nothing," and some are fast-paced "let's do lots of fun things." You may want a vacation where you sit on the beach and read, but that may not be the best memory for your kids. It might be fun for a bit, but then they'll get bored after a day or so. What I've tried to do is think through the snapshots that I want swirling around in their minds after the vacation is over. When we went to the Grand Canyon, I found a way for us to go down the Colorado River for just a one-day trip. But the one-day trip was a great memory.

Many of the memories you create may not be convenient or easy for you. They may not cost you much money, but they might cost sleep and sweat. Take, for example, the times I have gone camping with my son, Cameron. I have always tried to be a parent who says, "Hey, let's do this sometime," and then actually follows through on that statement. So when I tell Cameron, "Hey, let's camp out before it gets too cold," it really means we are going to do that. Fortunately, we live sort of in the country, which made it easier when he was smaller, because we could camp out in our back yard and he would be happy.

I remember one camping trip last year. Cameron and I went to a nearby lake. When we got there, we put our stuff in a boat and rowed to one side that had a waterfall and a cliff. We jumped off the cliff into the water and swam around. Later, we got back in the boat and rowed all the way across the lake. On the way, we caught three big mouth bass. We got to the other side, pitched our tent and cooked the fish over the camp-fire. After spending the night there, we got up and took a long hike— during which we ended up getting lost and having some adventures.

On the way back the next day, Cameron said the golden words that every parent wants to hear: "Pop, this was the best camping trip I've ever been on. In fact, I think it is one of the best times in my life so far." To me, nothing compared to the joy of being with my son, hearing those words, and creating a memory that will last a lifetime.

Remember when I mentioned late-night running with Charity? Let me tell you how it happened. Charity, my younger daughter, has become quite the runner. When she says, "Papa, let's go running," it's another way for her to say, "I want to spend time with you." I remember one night when I finished preaching at the end of a long day. We just finished a great ministry moment on our campus. At 11:00 P.M., on the way home, Charity says, "Hey, Papa, did you want to go running tonight?" That was the farthest thing from my mind and what I wanted least. I had an early morning the next day. But then I thought, *What a great way to create a memory, going running with my daughter at 11:30 P.M. and then talking on the way back.* I ended up going. Was I tired the next day? Yes! I don't remember what was so important, but she still remembers the night we went running at 11:30 P.M.

One of the things my daughter asked me that night was if I would be interested in training to run a marathon with her. When she asked me, I had no interest in doing that. I wanted to do it sometime in my life, but with the busyness of my traveling, I had no motivation for marathon training. But when I thought about how much time I would be spending with her, running and talking and sharing Scripture together, what a great memory we would have! This last year at home before she moves out, we can say that we trained to run a marathon together! Even as I'm writing this, we're beginning to train.

How You Respond to Bad News

There is bound to be some bad news sometime as you are raising your kids. How you respond to the news is critical. Sometimes parents say the most shockingly horrible things that, no matter what they do, cannot be rewound. The words just replay like film, over and over again. When my oldest daughter, Hannah, got in a terrible car accident with her first car, part of me was angry. *Why would she drive so fast on a slippery road?!* Yet, I knew that she was always going to remember my first response. What did I care about most—her or the car? I realized that how I responded on the phone and what I did when I first got on the scene would affect her for life. I could always go back later and talk about what had happened, but I could never replace that first memory.

Grades tend to bring out another huge opportunity to learn how to respond to bad news. There is always going to be challenging times when it comes to grades. It may be that your kids are heading in the wrong direction with grades, and you need to have a serious discussion. But what if your kid gets all *A*s and one *B*? Your response to that one *B* is also going to make a memory. If you say, "What happened? Why didn't you make an *A* in this class?" Or you say, "Why did you get a *B*?" instead of first saying, "Wow! What a great job you did," your child may think, *I can never do enough to please my mom (or dad)*. Even if there are a few lower grades that need to be discussed, there is an opportunity to comment on the grades that were good before you dissect the other issue at hand.

Rites of Passage Memories

When Hannah turned 13, we made an important statement to introduce her to such a special time in life. We wanted her teenage years to be exciting, full of life and memorable, not just a bunch of stressed-out, hateful experiences to get through. Every year we did something special and exciting to celebrate. Then our second daughter got the same gift when she turned 13.

Turning 13 was a special "rite of passage" for our girls. We just completed celebrating Cameron's thirteenth birthday. His special time was a little different, because he's a boy. With the girls, we took them on a date for a weekend of play and fun. But we also talked about some serious things and then presented them with a purity ring (a ring that signifies a pledge of sexual abstinence until marriage).

We spent several months in preparation for Cameron's birthday. Six months before his thirteenth birthday, I told him at a Bible study that I was going to start walking him down a path that would prepare him for manhood. From that point on, we met once a week for breakfast. He began to memorize Scripture and what the definition of what a man is, including the different ingredients of being a real man. I gave him symbolic gifts such as plaques and dog tags so that he could easily remember what he was learning.

When it came time for Cameron's actual birthday, we had something magnificent set up that we believed he would never forget. One thing we did was to present him with a genuine replica of a Brave Heart sword with a slogan he created in Latin inscribed on it: *semper deo habitato*. This means, "always for God will I live." We also incorporated a very memorable bonfire in the woods that night. At the fire, several men whom he looked up to and trusted each gave him symbolic gifts of what it means to be a man. He also got to eat the biggest steak he had ever seen.

We decided that we want to mark each year of our kids' teen years with a fantastic memory. At 14, each of our girls flew to her grandmother's for a weekend outing. At 15, each girl went on a special trip with Mom. At 16, each girl got to choose where in the U.S. she wanted to go for a weekend. Both of my girls wanted to take a friend to New York City. (It's a good thing I travel a lot to save up those frequent flyer miles!) When the girls turned 17, we gave each a shopping spree (with a limit). Each year, they remember more than a party; they remember the heritage we gave them. Sometimes, creating the memory required putting money away to make it happen, and sometimes it didn't require a cent.

With Cameron, I have tried to create different kinds of memories. We ride dirt bikes together. We go hunting. We go camping and fishing.

Some of our memories are of us getting lost in the woods while out camping. That memory was free; but all the talks, fun and frustration that we've had are priceless. We also have memories of getting lost on our dirt bikes and trying to pull a bike out of a ravine, in the rain. Of course, spending the time together provides a lot of life lessons and teachable moments.

My encouragement to you would be to make a list of things you want to do with your family to make some good memories. Make a list of things you will do as a family, where everyone is laughing and having a good time. Then make a list of ways to create individual memories with each of your kids. Make plans to do things on the list this year, this month, maybe even this week. Think about what is occupying their memory banks now. Then dream a little bit so that you can fill them with a library of great memories.

In every memory there is a message, whether good or bad. Recently, when I was in New York City, getting ready for a big event, I had the opportunity to meet Sean Hannity (of the Fox News show *Hannity and Colmes*) while I was there with Charity. After a few minutes, Sean asked, "Why don't you come on the show this afternoon? Let's talk about teenage behavior." He ended up having me debate with a woman on the air for 45 minutes. He asked Charity to speak as well, allowing her to share that moment with me. At the end of the interview, Sean said, "Why don't you come into the TV studio tonight? Franklin Graham and Rick Warren are going to be there." I looked at Charity and then at Sean and said, "I already have an appointment tonight; Charity and I are going to a show." He said, "Okay, that is fine, no problem."

Later that night, as Charity and I were walking down the street, I thought, *Man, I could have gone over there; I could have seen those two leaders again.* I could have developed a better relationship with Sean Hannity. Then I thought, *What is the best that might have come of it?* Perhaps another meeting with those two leaders and a TV appearance with Sean. Even if that happened, it would already be a distant memory. But had I said yes, I would have communicated to Charity that accepting Sean's invitation was more important than the date I had made with her. At that moment, I had the choice of planting a lingering bad memory or giving her a memory that told her, "You are more important than all the notable Christian leaders I could be spending time with."

Those kinds of memories are the ones that make our kids secure and open their hearts toward us. Those choices make them feel valued, which in turn increases their pliability when we attempt to shape them and pour our values into them. In every memory, there is a message. Make sure the memories you leave your kids contain the right kinds of messages.

A STRONG MARRIAGE = SECURE KIDS

So much has been said and written on the value of having a strong marriage. My wife and I have read many books by authors such as James Dobson, Bill Hybels, Gary Smalley and Dennis Rainey on the subject and have used their wisdom to build and strengthen our marriage. I'm not going to even try to reiterate those relationship principles here.

The point I do want to make in this chapter is that if we really want a chance at creating a culture in our home that is stronger than the culture of the world, we have to pay attention to the health of our marriage relationship. The *culture of a home emanates from the relationship between husband and wife* (for children, that's Mom and Dad). You can't pretend that loving your kids and being committed to them is the only thing that creates the culture. It's actually your relationship with your spouse that brings stability, confidence and wholeness to the home.

With so many divorces happening in our culture, it's not uncommon for young people, even our own children, to wonder if divorce is going to attack their home. Are Mommy and Daddy always going to stay together? This anxiety is breeding insecurity in children. If there are fights or disagreements, or if the *D*-word is ever used in a discussion or in a burst of anger, it only perpetuates this fear. The security that every child needs is not created just by saying, "Your mother and I will never get a divorce." The wholesomeness of a great romance and friendship (showing that you like as well as love each other) makes your kids feel safe and gives them confidence that their home will be stable and secure.

It's clear that children need *both* parents to have the healthiest up-bringing. I know that there are many single-parent families doing a valiant job at making things work in spite of the bad situation they've found themselves in. The data is irrefutable on how little boys and girls need their daddy around.[1] It takes a man *and* a woman to lead a family.

- 71 percent of pregnant teenagers lack a father.
- 90 percent of homeless and runaway children are from father-less homes.
- 85 percent of children who exhibit behavioral disorders come from fatherless homes.
- 71 percent of high school dropouts come from fatherless homes.[2]

Steps to a Healthy Relationship

In the following section, I'm going to give you some relevant tips that Katie and I have found to be critical to the success of our home.

Spend Time Together

After the new wears off of a marriage relationship, it's easy to start taking each other for granted. You stop pursuing each other. You get focused on all the busyness of raising children—getting them to do their homework, taking them to sports practices, games and other lessons and rehearsals. There is really no time left for each other. Nevertheless, husbands and wives need to prioritize their relationship in such a way that they make time for each other.

One of the things that Katie and I have done for years is have a weekly date night. We also learned very early in our relationship about having "couch time" every day. After I got home and said hi to the kids and loved on them, Katie and I would sit down and talk about how the day went, and so forth. The kids would see us spending time with each other even though they wanted our attention. They saw that we gave top priority to our relationship with each other.

It's important for children to see that they are not the center of your universe. If they are the center of your universe (which is common thinking of parenting romanticized), they control your world. They get you to do anything they want. What?! My spouse is more important than my kids? It might sound harsh or heartless, but the fact is, kids feel secure when they see a team of a mom and a dad who love each other and are committed to each other. The kids feel fine being priority number two.

Show a United Front with the Kids

There are many decisions that the two of you will disagree on. Katie and I made a decision early on that when we had kids, we would never disagree in front of them. As far as our kids were concerned, we were always in agreement with each other. If we needed to talk about something, we would talk apart from the kids.

A united front makes it almost impossible for kids to play Mom against Dad. If a child knows that Mom is okay with a decision, but Dad is not, the child can work the system. This united front commitment also allowed us to work things out in private, especially if it required some difficult and serious dialogue. Never verbalize disagreements in front of your kids. Even if you are the one who acquiesces and does not get your way, you still win, because as a team, you are both deciding to go the same direction.

Stand Up for and Support Each Other

Katie and I made a commitment that we would always be each other's greatest advocate. If my kids were saying something they didn't like about Mom, even if I agreed with what they might be saying, I stood up for her. I might say something like, "I know she has wisdom, and God gave her to you, and we are going to honor her." We always made each other look good for our kids.

Some small-minded moms and dads give in to the temptation to be liked. Even if they are not fueling their kids' grumbling, they are allowing derogatory words about the other parent to go unchallenged from the mouth of their teens. There is no advantage to the child feeling like one of you is the favorite parent.

Even in a divorce situation, with kids going back and forth between homes, there is no advantage to making the former spouse look bad. That person helped bring your child into the world. It's your responsibility to make your child's other parent look as wholesome as possible in the midst of a very difficult situation. Making yourself look better only benefits you, not the kids.

Do More Than Tolerate Your Spouse

Some have given in to the delusion of believing, "I will just put up with my spouse. I don't really like him (or her); but because I love my kids, we're staying together." While it sounds noble, if you really loved your kids, you would love your spouse too. You would work things out and humble yourself, and you and your spouse would listen to each other and let God help you win each other's heart back.

The best thing that you can do for your kids is to love your spouse with all your heart. Your children can sense whether there is wholesome, fervent, committed love in the home. You can say that you are staying together for the sake of the kids, but in reality, that's just a recipe for disaster. Every day there are stories of parents whose divorce, after their kids turned 18, 19, 20, 25, absolutely destroyed their children because they realized the delusion of their family life for all those years. Don't just endure for the sake of the kids; deal with the real issues and go to counseling if you need it. Ask God to draw your hearts toward each other once again.

Agree On Parenting Habits

Before Katie and I started having kids, we read books on how to parent. We both had come from divorced homes and did not have the best wisdom on how to raise kids. We sought people who were wiser than us. And there are plenty of them around.

Before you have children, develop a philosophy for parenting that you both agree on. This needs to include the issue of discipline—deciding on the behaviors that require consequences, and why. This is one of the reasons why two parents in a family are so important. As you are deciding how to parent and how to discipline, and what values you want to pour into your children, there are going to be times when one of you will be totally and completely exasperated. Your child has spun you in a web of his or her logic, and you feel helpless and frustrated. That is when your spouse can come in and help make sense of the situation. He or she is able to be a sounding board for you. You are a refuge for each other so that you can lead from a position of strength. Whoever is spun in the web is going to have blinders on, at best. The other parent offers a different perspective. Together you can confidently make decisions to move forward and resolve the issue with your child.

Moral Authority to Lead Your Family

The way you conduct your relationship with your spouse adds or detracts from your moral authority with your family. When you look at your kids and say, "This is the way I want us to live," is that standard reflected in your life? Do your kids see it lived in your relationship with your spouse? Do they see you reflecting the standard as an individual? If you scream or cuss at each other, why should your kids allow you to speak into their lives? You want to shape them with good values, critique their conduct and impart wisdom, and yet they see a problem with the way you live. Why would they want to embrace the values you are espousing? We would all like to say, "Do as I say, not as I do."

But that is exactly what Jesus said about the Pharisees. The truth is, children look to us and do what we do much more than they do what we say. As the saying goes, "More is caught than taught."

What if you are from a divorced and/or blended family? How do you discipline the kids from your spouse's first marriage? How do you make sure there is wisdom being used between the biological parent and the stepparent? If you're struggling with these issues, I encourage you to read one of the books listed here:

- *Blended Families: Creating Harmony as You Build a New Home Life* by Maxine Marsolini
- *The Smart Step-Family* by Ron L. Deal
- *Winning the Heart of Your Stepchild* by Dr. Bob Barnes

It's the biological parent who needs to do most of the disciplining of his or her children in a mixed family situation. You don't ever want to put the stepchild in a position where he or she would say, "You are not my real parent; you can't say that to me." If fact, if there is a stepfather, much of the discipline might have to come through the mother. Even though Scripture says the man is the head of the home, you have a different situation. The stepfather can support the mom, but to keep from dividing the family further and living in a hellacious world, the biological parent should always do the disciplining and the correcting.

One last word of encouragement to husbands: When your children see that you love your wife and are pursuing her, it provides an example for your sons of what a wholesome love looks like so that they will see a glaring difference in what the world calls love. Your little girls will see what a wholesome romantic love looks like so that they are not enticed and lured by guys who tell them they are pretty and that they love them, just so they can use them. There are so many intangibles created by a strong marriage. It builds security in the hearts of young people and helps them make decisions not out of fear but in response to the examples their parents show of a wholesome, thriving romance that makes them want to have the same.

To raise kids effectively, there is a lot of coaching, mentoring, rebuking and disciplining involved. If, in the middle of trying to discipline your child, you are constantly dealing with a battle between you and your spouse as well, you are not going to have near the effectiveness of shaping your young people that you could have. Much of what you say will be disregarded, because it doesn't line up with the way you are living. A solid, thriving marriage relationship builds a culture of trust and confidence so that you can pour your values into your children and they will receive your teaching, because they see the benefits in your own marriage.

NO SUBSTITUTE FOR ONE ON ONE

In my ministry, I tend to have more on my to-do list than I could possibly ever get done. So when I started traveling when my children were very young, I always took one of my children with me.

My initial concept of how to be a father with a child traveling with me was to keep her occupied with a few toys, give her a bottle when she was hungry, change her diaper when needed and get lots of work done while on the plane. As long as I could keep her occupied and tears-free, I could multitask. Of course, I also played with my child, but I always had one eye and most of my thoughts on all the work I still needed to get done.

This travel plan changed about the time my children turned two. At that point, when I held my child, talked to her and jostled her while I looked at email or read something, she began talking to me in baby-talk language, trying to communicate. That's when just occupying her time was not enough. She wanted to have a "conversation" with me.

At some point, between ages two and three, I remember that each of my kids would grab my face and turn it toward her as I held a pseudo conversation while working. The first time that happened, my temptation was to continue reading and try to keep my child occupied. But in my heart, I felt the rebuke. Was I going to be a father who did the letter of the law, but not the spirit of the law? Sure, I was trying to be a good father by taking my child with me. I would change a diaper and do all the work of a father traveling with a child, but I wasn't really doing the spirit of the law and being engaged. I thought, *What a tragedy it would be to have my kids grow up traveling with me but never having one-on-one interaction with me.* Supposedly, this was the reason I was taking them with me.

There is no substitute for one-on-one time with your children, on a regular basis. It's easy to think, *I can just do a whole family outing.* Family vacations and dinners are great. Playing as a family is great. But each person has his or her own challenges, frustrations and insecurities. When you get one on one and talk, you optimize the opportunity to truly engage your child's heart at a deeper level.

Being with a group of people called your family, all the time, can be difficult. Even though it's family, no one gets enough individual attention. The average father only spends 6.5 hours of time with his kids each week, and mothers spend 12.9 hours.[1] All children are different from one another, and we need to pay individual attention to them.

As I have already mentioned, your kids will like to do different things one on one, so develop a list of what each child likes to do with Mom or Dad. Maybe it's shopping, having tea or coffee out, playing music or taking a walk together. There is really no substitute for these one-on-one times. As you spend time together, you can share your heart and what is really going on with you. As you do that, your kid will begin to share his or her heart. There is a feeling of reciprocity. You opened up, and now he or she feels like it's okay to be vulnerable as well.

I would encourage you to begin one-on-one time even when your children are very young—three or four years old. Dads, don't ever go anywhere without one of your kids with you. This even includes runs to the hardware store. This is time that you could spend alone, but take one of your kids and have a conversation about things that are simple but important topics.

A parent's common excuse is, "I just don't have time to spend one on one." My answer to that is, "Do you have time for therapy?" Do you have time to take your kids every week for three years to somebody who can help them and talk through issues with them? So many of life's "common" problems can be solved by having a sounding board, and you want to be sure that you're that sounding board for your child.

One study I learned about when I was doing my master's degree in counseling/psychology compared a rabbi, a priest, a psychologist and a friend (I know, this sounds like a joke) for their effectiveness in helping a person talk through a problem. What was the difference in effectiveness between a person going to a professional such as a rabbi, priest or psychologist for help versus talking to a really good friend? The study found that there is actually *no difference.* Think of the significance of that—a friend is just as good at helping someone through his or her problem as a trained psychologist with a Ph.D.[2]

What people need is a friend—someone to share their heart with. We all have a need to share our hearts, but we tend to only do that one on one. When people go to a psychiatrist, they are really paying someone to do what a parent, friend or spouse could do.

When we get into a regular rhythm of meeting with our kids one on one, it doesn't always have to be intense. But you must proactively create an environment where they will feel like they want to share their heart. If you don't ever set that up, the heart-sharing will never happen. This is reciprocity. You listen to them; they will want to listen to you. You share you heart, and they will share theirs.

Listen to your child's heart, even if he or she talks a really long time. Be careful to guard yourself from the temptation to jump in and correct, coach or fix everything. Let your child talk! A major part of her need is to be able to talk it out. She may not want a logical answer; she may just need for you to hear her. If you wait to give advice, you might even go away and come back with better thoughts on what to share than if you tried to fix the problem immediately.

We as parents want, and need, to be *the relational center of our kids' lives.* We don't want them sharing their hearts with friends, with a blog or in a gang. The only way we are going to be the one they go to is if we create lots of one-on-one time. If at first your child is not comfortable one on one, think of fun and adventurous things to do together; They will soon begin to look forward to your time together. I guarantee it; they will come around. Spend a little bit of money, but more than that, spend the time to do the one-on-one activities. Your children will benefit from having the relational center of their life be how they connect to you, not to other people.

You may be saying, "Okay, Ron, but what about a Goth-dressing, Satan-worshiping cynical teen? How do you get through to one of those young people?" Well, I recently had the opportunity to do that when his parents sent him to me for the summer to "fix" him. They were exasperated, having done "all they could do" to get through to him. The first day, I took him to breakfast, and he told me he worshiped Satan, and he knew I was going to try to get him close to God, and he was informing me that it was never going to happen, I didn't look shocked or try to cram Jesus down his throat. I just said, "Hey, do you like to ride dirt bikes?"

His face lit up. A few days later, we went riding. We went to lunch several times. We went jet-skiing together and laughed, played and had small talk. Little by little, he began to open up about his life, his family and his heart. I took him on trips out of town (like I do with my own kids). He shared a little more. Before the summer was over, he had committed his life to Jesus, renounced Satan, was reading the Bible like crazy and had forgiveness in his heart toward his parents. All it took was time and love.

Parents who say, "I have done everything I can do" should rethink that statement. These parents wanted me to "fix" their son. All I did was what they should have done all along: spend time one on one with him. Maybe you have done everything except the thing your child needs the most: time one on one with you.

YOUR KIDS TRUMP YOUR CAREER AND MINISTRY

We were enjoying the first day of our one-week Florida getaway as a family. The kids were buzzing with all the fun we were going to have—from going to the beach to visiting Disney World. In the middle of the hotel lobby, I got a phone call from someone inviting me to come to a special meeting with him and the president of the United States, George W. Bush. While I listened to this call, I was looking at my family in the lobby, so excited about what we were planning to do. I told the person that I was in Florida on my family vacation. He said, "But, Ron, this is a two-hour meeting with the president of the United States." I said, "I know that, but I'm on my vacation with my family." He repeated his last statement. After a few minutes of discourse, this very kind gentleman realized that nothing could dissuade me from spending time with my family, even a meeting with the president.

As I listened to what he was saying, I played in my mind the memory my kids would have and the message I would have sent them if I had given in to the desire to go meet with the president. Sure, my family would have forgiven me. Katie would have said, "Sure, honey, you can go." There may or may not have been another opportunity to meet with the president, but there would never be another opportunity to raise my kids. There would never be another opportunity for this vacation. I had one chance to leave an indelible mark in their mind of the value that I place on them.

When my wife told the kids that I chose to spend time with them over meeting with the president, there is no amount of preaching or saying "I love you" that could possibly compare with the value they felt at that moment.

All of us are busy people. If you have a career, are involved in ministry, or have a desire to succeed in some kind of endeavor, there are always going to be other things to do to keep you away from your kids. You have to make a decision *in advance* that your spouse and children are more important to you than your career and/or ministry. Period! When you make that decision, many other decisions will fall into place, including where you spend your time and invest your heart. When "opportunities" come up, your priorities are already set. You may think, *I'll get promoted if I make this presentation really good and work over the weekend.* But you also know that it's your son's first T-Ball game. There will always be another opportunity for promotion, but there will never be another first T-ball game. If you are in ministry, there will be another TV appearance or great church to preach in, but you will never get a chance to raise your kids again.

We need to be careful that our drive to succeed in business and ministry does not justify neglecting or overlooking the precious young ones God has given us to raise.

Be There!

You need to make a decision that there are some things you are just not going to miss:

- You are not going to miss birthdays.
- You are not going to miss drama performances.
- You are not going to miss games. If a child has 30 games in a season, it's okay to miss a few. But don't be an absent father or mother.
- You are not going to miss celebrating your wedding anniversary.

I can think of opportunities that came up at the same time as a family birthday or anniversary. It seemed like this opportunity might never come my way again, but I had already made the decision about what I would not miss for the sake of my family. I don't even mention most of these opportunities to my family, because it would be easy for them to feel bad (because they don't want to mess up Dad's career). And I have tried to avoid promising, "I'll make it up to you later." There are some things you just can't make up. You send a bigger statement by just making sure that you are there for your family.

You don't have to be a perfect parent. If you are just *there* and have a real relationship with your kids, it makes up for a lot of things that may not be so perfect. There will always be another big break, another deal to make, another promotion to go for; but you have only one chance to raise your kids. They will remember where you spent your time. They will remember if you sacrificed for your family.

But I Meant to Be There . . .

Famous words from a parent with good intentions: "I meant to be at your ballgame . . . I meant to be at your recital . . . I meant to be at your parent-teacher conference . . ." Are these words supposed to comfort the young person who sees every other parent but theirs at an event? We easily say the words, "I really *wanted* to be there." Think about that for a second. Did you REALLY want to be there? Whatever we really want to do, we do. When we tell our kids that we wanted to be there but could not make it, we are telling them we *wanted to be somewhere else more*, and that is why we were somewhere else. In a kid's mind, all he is thinking is that if you really wanted to be there, you would have been there. There are only a few situations when absence from a child's event is unavoidable, when not being there is because of an emergency. When we say, "I really wanted to be there, but . . ." we are sending a message that we didn't want to be there as much as we wanted our career or our ministry.

Decide in Advance

Make the decision in advance that you are going to give top priority to your spouse and your children. Does that mean there can't be some massaging of this rule? Of course not; but I hesitate to even say that. Many families live from one compromise to another. They make a rule or decision and then they violate it repeatedly for the rest of their life.

If you make the decision in advance, missing out on an opportunity that comes your way is not such a hard thing to stomach. I did not get a chance to meet with President Bush, but I did get a chance to meet with my family. I lived according to my values. My kids love me, and I love them. I have decided what type of marriage and family I want, and everything else will have to revolve around that. I made the decision to not cheat my family long before I got the call to meet with the president.

We have always had a weekly family day or family date. Flexibility comes into play if for some reason I have to travel during our regular time together. Then we find another family time that week. If I work an extra day during my regular day off, I find another day to "give back" to the family. Katie does not have to beg me, or even ask. I just plan it into my life. I have tried to live so that my kids would never say, "But, Dad, you are never here," even though I travel every week all over the country. In fact, I would say that as my kids grew up, I actually spent more time with them than many fathers who never travel out of town. At the end of the day, when your kids are teenagers, and they still give you great big hugs, you realize it was no sacrifice at all.

Coming Home from Work

It's so important that when you come home, you come home both physically *and* mentally. Many people come home from work so exhausted physically that they are not any good to their family. Their mind is still at work. They are sitting there with the kids thinking about what they are going to do the next day. Maybe they turn the TV on and get engaged in their favorite program and call that spending time with family.

When you go to work, you put your game face on. You work hard. When you get home from work, it's the second half of your workday; it's not over. It's over when the kids are in bed. Your wife may have been working hard all day. Now is the time for the *family work* of being a parent. You focus and mentally engage. Turn off work; leave it in your briefcase. Don't check your email. Engage with your kids. Roll around the floor. Laugh with them. Play with them. Do stupid things with them.

I remember when my kids were smaller—and even now that they are older—that I would tickle them, play with them, laugh with them, wrestle with them and listen to them. Closing my eyes at the end of an intense day and listening to their giggles and laughter as I tickled them on the floor would be like a waterfall over my soul just soothing away all the intensity of the day. It created balance in my life.

Your life is not all about your job. It is not all about your ministry. But it is all about the different dimensions that God has allowed you to participate in. If you have children, that is one dimension. There is something about a child's laughter, and comforting them when they are hurting, and listening to their little hearts that brings wholesomeness to you as an adult.

You know that if you don't go to work with your game face on and give your very best, you are in danger of being fired. It's the same at home. If you don't come home and put your game face on and give your very best, you are in danger of being *fired by your kids*. They will fire you from being the one they share their heart with. They will fire you from being the one they cuddle up to. They will fire you from being the one they trust with all their heart. *I would rather be fired from my job than fired from my family.*

The Gift of Family

It's easy to think, *If I put my family first, I am getting further behind; I have a list of things to do at my job (or ministry) that takes 24/7 to do.* It really is a fallacy to think that way. In order to do your very best at your job or ministry, you need to be whole. You need to be strong. You need to have a whole family, whole children and a whole relationship with your spouse. By listening to them, disciplining, instructing, talking, running, being frustrated—just being present with them, you become a better person. When you go back to your office, you are not just a driven machine executing details; you are equipped to relate better to the people you are managing and deal with the frustrations they have at home.

It's one-dimensional living to only go after your career or ministry. We often think that if we stay focused on that one dimension, we will be successful. If you are married, having a wholesome marriage will make you more successful than just being driven by your career. If you have children, being focused on your marriage and your children brings wholesomeness to your life so that when you put your game face on for work, you really are at 100 percent capacity rather than barely surviving from day to day.

Marrying Katie has truly saved my life. In order to have a balanced, wholesome marriage, I have learned that I've got to listen to her. I've learned how to say to myself, *It's time to shut work off and focus on her.* When we decided to have children, we committed to spending the right amount of time with them. Family life has actually preserved my life and increased my chances of living a longer life because of the wholesomeness found in a relationship with my wife and children.

Don't miss out on the experience of having your kids share something that enlightens you, or even rebukes you. They may show you a part of your personality that needs work. They will definitely give you joy. God brings our children into our life to make us the whole people we need to be to be effective in the world, period.

SHOW ME DA MONEY, AND I'LL SHOW YOU WHAT YOU VALUE

It could not be more revealing: What you spend your money on reflects what you think is important. We either invite or repel the world's culture with every dollar we spend.

I mentioned at the beginning of this book that teenagers spend $150 billion a year on what you allow them to spend it on. Please don't make the mistake of thinking, *They earned it; they can buy whatever they want*. You, as the parent, have the right to say, "No, you are not ready for an iPod [or a computer]." You allow them to work a summer job, and then you help them plan how to spend the money wisely. For example, our kids had to save half of what they earned during the summer for college or for a car later on. If they wanted to buy something, they could save up the other half to get what they wanted (as long as we approved). They whined, but it taught them to save.

When PlayStation 3 was released right before Christmas 2006, a number of parents went on a spending frenzy in hopes of getting one for their child. Other people purchased the units to sell them on eBay and make a profit. The cheapest gaming console listed on the site sold for $4,300, with an average price between $7,000 and $10,000 (the highest bid was $30,000).[1]

Spending $30,000 on a gaming console priced at $450 is a sure sign that kids influence their parents' spending patterns. There is a lot of money spent on our kids. The question is, when they start putting the squeeze on you, who has influenced them to influence you? With the constant barrage of media luring them down a path, it's easy for the world's values to dominate most kids' desires.

Don't spend "guilt money" on your kids because you are not around enough and you are constantly trying to make up for it. Money will not make up for your absence. Don't succumb to all of your kids' demands for things their friends have told them they must have. Take control of the culture that you allow into the house by what you spend money on.

Our desire to give our kids more than what we had when growing up can lead to their absorption with the media that destroys them. Whether you put TVs in every room or get every latest gadget possible, many times, in trying to make life better for them, we actually make it worse. You may actually be inviting a wall to be built between you and your kids. The time they spend and the values they learn from the media contraptions you bring home will actually put you farther away from having a deep relationship with them. Your desire to give them what you never had may turn out to be a curse and drive you farther apart as a family.

More Distractions for the Dollar

Let's get this straight. We want to have a great family. We want to focus our kids on the right values. We want to make sure they are not captured and taken away by the world's culture. Yet it's easy for us to send conflicting messages by the things we buy.

We need to think carefully about the impact of the dollars we spend. We can't just think, "I have always wanted this big flat screen," or "I had to get a satellite dish." Most of our spending is to appease our own ego and selfish desires or to appease someone whining for it. Sure, we can say we will have great times around the TV set. And that might happen once in a while; there may be some great conversations started from time to time. But how much positive family time do you get when you are allowing someone else to entertain you and shape your values non-stop? Just spending the money every month on your cable bill alone may cause you to feel obligated to watch it, otherwise you're wasting your money.

Interactive Games (Not Video Games)

I am not a real big game person myself. I am like everyone else who lets their brain go numb while watching something entertaining, especially after trying some games that weren't competitive enough. Board games were fun for an "unsophisticated generation," like when I grew up. Now it seems we have a very sophisticated society, and we need to be attentive to that. Video games fit the bill, right? Maybe, maybe not.

Video games can be very addictive. There is data that shows that many people who start gaming when they are young continue into their 20s and 30s. They spend endless hours playing really competitive games that lead to nothing. Of course, there are video games that you can play against each other in the living room, but that interactive playing may or may not happen, even though that is the intention. There are some other really good interactive board games that will engage your kids' attention, such as Mad Gab, Catch Phrase, Apples to Apples, Imagine If, Clue, Scattergories and Monopoly. And there are lots of great card games that are fun and force you to think and engage with your kids: UNO, Phase 10, Pit, Spoons, Hearts, Spit, Hit the Deck and Skip Bo, to name several.

You can create some great memories while playing interactive games or reading funny books aloud. We used to read at the dinner table. I remember laughing about a story we were reading and discussing the issues the story brought up.

Try to stay away from having every family night be about watching a video. That is the easy way out. There are always so many movies to pick from, and we ourselves have had to guard against only watching videos on family night. Think about an indulgent time spent absorbing Hollywood's values versus laughing hysterically together throughout a competitive game. Which would you choose?

Sometimes you all just need to relax and let your hair down. But if you get into the habit of doing that, and not engaging your kids, you will end up with 16-, 17- and 18-year-old couch potatoes absorbed by media because all their family time was spent silently in front of a viewing screen.

House Choice

All the things that used to be luxuries have turned into necessities and must-haves. Now 8-, 9- and 10-year-olds have cell phones! It's okay to say no to cell phones. We felt pressure from our own kids to get them CD players and cell phones when they were younger than we thought they should be to own these things. We told them no. They had to wait until they were 16 to get a cell phone. Proverbs 23:4 says, "Do not wear yourself out to get rich; have the wisdom to show restraint." Just because you can afford stuff does not mean that you should buy it for your home, or for your children.

We have prioritized putting money away for our kids' college, for a rainy day, for the future, to give to missions. There are many things we could give money to rather than just indulging our kids and ourselves. Using your money to give away (like tithing to your church) and giving to missionaries and relief agencies such as Compassion International will send a positive message to your kids and instill the value of being a good steward of the monetary resources God has provided. We have supported two Compassion International kids since they were small and sent and received letters to them for our kids to read as they grew up.

Every dollar you spend communicates what you value. Even if you can afford everything you want (or everything your kids want), it may be smarter to refrain from fulfilling those desires. Do not let innovation and technology drive your purchases. Make decisions on what you spend money on *based on what you value* and what is important to you. Before you buy, think through the implications of purchasing a piece of technology, which could turn into a time thief and shape the wrong values. If that means you don't get the flat screen TV that you've wanted for years, then so be it.

Fathers and mothers who get a monetary bonus from their employer and spend that money on indulging themselves on cutting-edge technology only make the family even more chaotic by inviting more media into the house. Before you buy, think about the effect every purchase will have on your family. Have the wisdom to show restraint. Owning every toy that has been invented is not the path to freedom and happiness. You need to decide in advance what kind of family you want to have and the values you want them to emulate. Then allow your purchases to line up with those values. Even though your ego will not be thrilled in the moment, your family will be thrilled in the long term.

TEACHING YOUR KIDS TO BE DREAMERS

In chapter 2, I mentioned that 98 percent of people are followers; 2 percent are the shapers of culture. The 2 percent are the dreamers. One of our biggest responsibilities as parents is not only to protect our kids from culture but to help them be the shapers of culture. A lot of this book so far has shown you how to insulate your kids and proactively instill your values in them. The point of doing that is not just so you can have a "good family" with great values, but to teach your family to take those values and begin to impact and shape the rest of the world.

How do we get our kids into the 2 percent who are the shapers of culture? How do we get them to be the dreamers for their generation, inventing the gadgets, writing the songs, driving the businesses, running for political office and sitting on school boards? It starts while they are young. As moms and dads, we need to be about the business of sparking the desire and planting the seed in their heart to creatively dream when they are very, very young.

We have told our kids from the beginning that they were born to change the world. They were born to make a difference. We put them to sleep at night praying over them, "God, use Hannah (Charity, Cameron) to change the world. Use her to make a difference . . . to touch people's lives." From the youngest age, that seed was planted in their minds and hearts; they grew up believing they really can change the world and make a difference.

Our goal as parents is not just for our kids to become "good" members of society. We need to raise them to be change agents. We need to raise them to take the values we have instilled in them, harnessed with a passion for God, and inspire them to reach out to people. We multiply the impact we have had on their lives to countless others, as they reach out. Let me give you some practical ways that you can do this for your kids.

Teaching Your Kids to Change the World

Encourage Them to Be Others-Oriented

From a very young age, encourage your children to be "others-oriented." For example, when your kids decide to get entrepreneurial, as most kids will, you can encourage them to mow lawns and sell lemonade so that they can donate the money to help *other* people, not just satisfy their own purchasing power. In a similar vein, when they do want things, instead of buying them everything they want, teach them to find enterprising ways of earning money. They need to learn how to save for things they want to buy.

Help Them Pursue Small Dreams

We can teach our children to be opportunistic. When my oldest daughter, Hannah, was 13, she had an idea that she wanted to use the Internet to help preteen girls through a website she wanted to create. I got a mentor to help her learn how to do a little bit of programming. She wrote the code for a website called girlofgod.com. She had all kinds of ideas on how she was going to do the art. It was thrilling. She got lots of preteen girls on that site and ministered to them. The vision did not continue for very long, but it was a fantastic life lesson for her. She saw this truth: "If I have a dream, I can learn how to go about achieving it, and I can accomplish something." Help your kids find opportunities to impact other people and not just indulge themselves; and then show them how to take the vision from an idea stage to completion.

Defy Selfish Logic

All throughout our kids' growing-up years, we had a special Christmas morning tradition. After eating breakfast, we got ready to leave the house for what my wife and I felt was one of our most important holiday traditions before opening gifts: We would serve the meal at the local Salvation Army. We did this to send a message to our children that Christmas is about serving, not just indulging ourselves. Inevitably, we would end up having some conversations with people who were really hurting, listening to them and praying for them. Look for various ways to plant seeds in your kids about being others-centered.

Out-of-the-Box Experiences

One of the greatest things you can do is help your kids want to serve and impact other people. You can provoke this by giving them experiences that are way out of the box. Sending them to summer camp is great, but finding a camp that doesn't indulge them makes a bigger impact. Look for something that teaches them to be closer to God or gain a skill. Some examples would be leadership camp like Student Leadership University, basketball camp, acting camp or anything that will give them a skill they can use even in their high school years to serve others and become excellent at something.

One of the greatest things you can do is help your kids go on a missions trip in another part of the world. There they can see how other people live who are far less fortunate than we are in America. Start doing this at a young age. (We started taking kids on Global Expedition trips with Teen Mania when they were 11 years old.)

If MTV is targeting kids at younger and younger ages, then so must we. We must plant in our kids a desire to really make a difference and change the world. Sending them on a missions trip is not just sending them on the trip. It's showing them how they can raise money. Of course the trip is not just paid for by Mom and Dad; the kids have to write fund-raising support letters and get sponsors. They have to prepare. They have to bring their passport, pack their clothes and be responsible. It gets them out of their comfort zone.

While on a Global Expeditions trip, they are mentored and discipled (taught precepts and principles about a godly life based on the teaching of Scripture). At the same time, they are reaching out in a very practical way, whether that means digging a well in India or reaching out to orphans in Africa whose parents have died of AIDS. They realize that life is more than the stuff they accumulate. Even though they may not become a missionary later in their life, at least this experience gives them a taste of doing something that is definitely not self-centered.

Letting our children have this experience is a test for us as parents, a test of our trust that God will take care of our kids. Allowing them to go out of the country sends our children a message while they are young that they were born for greatness and destined to impact the world!

Katie and I began to take our kids on missions trips while they were very small—in fact, while they were still in the womb. But even when they were 1, 2 and 3 years old, we took them with us to different missions destinations so that they could see how the teenagers we took on the trips were doing. We always got them involved, even when they were only 4 or 5 years old. Sometimes they would take some of their toys or stuffed animals to give away to the children they met on the trips, while at other times they would say to a child through a translator, "Hey, I brought this doll for you and just wanted to let you know Jesus loves you." Our children would share things like this as they were giving their toys to the children of the world. Each step of the way—in every trip they took to Africa with me or to India with Katie—it made an impression on them. These indelible memories marked them for life through lessons of how blessed we are in America and how God created us to change the world.

When our kids were 11, they started going on missions trips by themselves. What this really meant was that they were accompanied by trained and refined leaders and with a team of kids their own age. This was an experience that they could have without Mom or Dad hovering over them. Now, this was as big a step of faith for us as it is for the thousands of parents who let their kids go every year on these trips. In fact, it was shocking for us to think that they were going to these nations with other leaders, even though they had been on trips many times with us.

I remember when Hannah first went on a junior missions trip to Costa Rica at age 11. It was amazing to hear her stories afterward. In fact, when she got back from her two-week trip, she sat down in my office for two hours and shared story after story of the miracles that had happened and how the Lord used her to minister to other children. At the end of our conversation, her lips began to quiver and her eyes filled with tears. She exclaimed, "Papa, I just feel like God wants to use me to do something to reach my generation!" With that said, she began to sob uncontrollably.

Even though Hannah grew up surrounded by a ministry and traveled to other countries, there was absolutely nothing I could have said that would have produced that response. It was only when Katie and I let her go minister for herself that God ignited the destiny inside her heart. From that moment on, she realized she was not just here on this earth for fun, but that God had placed her here for a reason. Your kids will experience the same thing when you find opportunities to get them out of the box so that God can ignite the destiny inside them.

Make Friends with Dreamers

I have said this in so many ways, but let me say it again: You *can* influence who your kid's friends are. Many parents think, *I can't influence anything my kid does at school.* That is not true.

You can influence who your kids' friends are even when they are at school. First of all, when they are young, plant in their heart the desire to have the right kinds of friends. That does not always mean they are going to choose correctly, so you are going to have to help shape who they call, who they hang out with, who they are allowed to interact with after school, which is where most of the shaping would happen. Most important, if you find kids who are really making a positive difference, find ways to get your kids connected with them. At the very least, do not allow them to have a bunch of slug friends that are so submerged with media and the culture that it rubs off on your kids.

Limit Media Input

The more they watch other people's media, the more they are part of other people's dreams. At the most, it can pour bad values into them. At the very least, it preoccupies their mind so that they are not dreaming and thinking, *What can I do in my school? What can I do this summer to change the world? What should I major in? What is my part in helping broken humanity?*

Give Rewards

Establish incentives for good grades, creativeness, demonstrating good character, and so on. Reward your kids with words, money, encouragement, opportunities, going out to do something fun together. If our value system is really about family values, and we really want them to be creative people, then let's reward the things we know are going to send our kids down that road. Inevitably, too many families reward what is not geared toward making their kids into innovators, shapers and creative people.

Inspire with Stories

I urge you to constantly share stories of historic greats or young people today who have done amazing things to shape our nation. You can read a story quickly during dinner time. A couple of books with examples of young role models are *Columbine Courage* and *The Power of One*. These books contain many stories about young people who have stood up for their faith. *The Power of One* also includes some biblical examples you can use to inspire your kids to be world changers.

Ultimately, your kids are your heritage to the world. Planting seeds in them from a very early age to use their life to change the world is our primary job. As we stay focused on the belief that "My job is to help them dream God's dream for them and do all I can to equip them to accomplish that dream," then we will all have children who impact the world much more than we have.

SECTION II

RECREATING A CULTURE IN YOUR CHURCH THAT OVERWHELMS THE WORLD

Now that we've examined how to recreate a culture in our family that will withstand the world, it's imperative that we turn our thinking to our church. There are a lot of families in your community with kids who need to be reached. The kids in those families, as well as the kids in Christian families, need to know that there is a peer group and a place they can go that embraces and affirms what they believe and, indeed, encourages them to continue on. It's not a matter of just getting kids to go to church. The question when they get there is, *What do they get?* We can beg them or force them to come on Sunday, but what can we do to create an environment where they actually *want* to be there? As we have already seen, parents have forced kids to go to church all their life and yet not truly influenced the way they believe or live.

As you read the next several chapters, whether you're a well-meaning parent or a church leader, please fully engage in this section of the book. All of us, as members of the Body of Christ, owe it to the younger generation to give them a fair chance at not just having faith, but thriving in their faith. We must create a place in our local churches where they are free to be passionate about God and they love coming for their growth and to get real answers to the questions they're asking about life.

ONE GENERATION AWAY FROM EXTINCTION

Judges 2:10 tells us that a generation rose up after Joshua and his generation had died that *knew not the Lord or the miracles that He had done.* Think about that for a moment. Think of Moses and all the miracles that God performed through him as he led the children of Israel out of slavery in Egypt—the parting of the Red Sea and all the plagues that had come on Egypt before that. Most of those people who came out of Egypt had died by the time Joshua and Caleb took over leadership after Moses' death. Under Joshua's leadership, there was another series of miracles: the drying up of the Jordan as the people crossed the river, the falling of the walls of Jericho, battle after battle that the Israelites won through the hand of God.

Now the Israelites actually were in the Promised Land they had been talking about for so long; they had the favor of God. They went into the land and settled into the blessing God had given them. However, this new generation did not know the Lord or the miracles that got them there.

I wonder if we're in a similar scenario in the United States of America. The Christian founders of our land who worked so hard to give us a land of religious freedom are marginalized at best. People who fought and died so that we would have a place for the gospel to thrive would be shocked at what thrives here instead. There are so many miracles that brought us a government that became an economic superpower because God blessed us so that we could be a blessing to the world.

Now that we have received our blessing, a new generation has risen up that expects this to be a land of privilege where they deserve every blessing they have. By the way, secular people wouldn't believe that God has anything to do with their blessings. We're in perilous danger of having the same epitaph as Israel at this juncture in America's life: *a generation grew up that knew not what God has done.*

What About the Five Percent?

You may have heard something about the next generation of Americans: Only 5 percent of them will be Bible-believing Christians.[1] In my book *Battle Cry for a Generation,* I clearly outlined the data regarding these numbers. Even though some would dispute the 5 percent, what is irrefutable is that the percentage is lower than it has ever been in the history of America. Of course, when we say 5 percent, there are more people than that who go to church, but we're talking about people who actually believe that the Bible is the Word of God and that we ought to take our direction from it, just like a compass. The Bible is not a book of opinions or a book of suggestions; it's a book of instructions from God for our lives. It provides absolutes to live by.

Other studies validate similar kinds of phenomena in the United States. For example, The American Church Research project found that the percentage of people who attended a Christian church in the last weekend is far below what most pollsters say.[2] George Barna and others say that the number of people who attend a Christian church is actually at 47 percent, but when you look at actual numbers, it looks like only 17.3 percent of people in our nation actually go to church.[3] In addition, The American Church Research Project has found that the percentage of people attending a Christian church each weekend decreased significantly from 1990 to 2006. It went from 20.6 percent in 1990 to 17.3 percent in 1995.[4] In the United States, some churches shut down and some churches are started each year, but when you do the math, we're losing between 3,500 and 4,000 churches a year.[5]

Think about what this says about the potential future of our nation. This is especially alarming when you consider the rise of atheistic books in pop culture that present the mention of God as idiocy. In March 2008, Oprah Winfrey started one of the largest churches in the world when she introduced Eckhart Tolle's *A New Earth* to her book club—a book that cheapens the deity of God to a mere "feeling."[6] There are many other atheistic books that add to our culture's view that Jesus was only a great man of our history, such as *The God Delusion* by Richard Dawkins. The 2004 movie *Saved!* should have alarmed every Evangelical Christian. The blatant and bold look at God and the Church was a reality check, as the movie was based on the view that many nonbelievers have of Christianity.[7] The way that Christians and churches are made fun of in the popular media, it's no wonder we're seeing these numbers.

Implications

If we think about the implications, before too long we're looking at the very real possibility of a post-Christian America. Indeed, from many perspectives, for those who want to make the argument, we're already post-Christian. But we're about ready to enter into a land of post-Christianity that we've never even imagined.

Think of post-Christian Europe—the thousands of cathedrals that are empty every Sunday morning all across the land and the horrific laws they make or even consider making. For example, in Germany they are considering making a law that once you're married, it only lasts seven years.[8] In England, there's nudity in regular newspapers.[9] In the Netherlands, there is an integration test that people must pass to become residents. Individuals are forced to observe affectionate homosexuals and women dressed inappropriately, with the warning that if they can't accept it, the Netherlands is not the right place for them.[10] In France, a daily news program called "Naked News" is pitched as "the program with nothing to hide." You guessed it—in the program all of the anchors present the news in the buff.[11]

There are other implications for going into a post-Christian America. Think about the monetary support for missions. When Brother K. P. Yohannan, the founder of Gospel for Asia, found out about the 5 percent, he called me and said, "Ron, do you realize what it's going to do to the mission's giving if we end up with only 5 percent of people as Bible-believing followers of God? What's going to happen to evangelism around the world?"

You should think about the media presence we have around the world. When people around the world think of America, they think of life portrayed in such TV shows as *Baywatch* or *Desperate Housewives*. They think of MTV and its velocity of horrific music, videos and other media coming out of our nation, destroying a young generation of a billion teenagers from around the world. (MTV is presently in 169 nations in 28 languages.[12])

I've received letters and emails from pastors around the world, saying, "Ron, we're losing our kids and we don't know what to do. They're more a part of your [United States] culture than they are of ours. Will you come here and help us reach the young people in our nation?" Recently, CNN produced a special called "God's Warriors" that talked about the whole BattleCry movement of how we are trying to rescue kids from the influence of advertisers and pop culture. I was contacted by a member of Italy's parliament; the message was, "We've got a battle for our young people here. Can you come here and help us learn how to reach the young people in Italy?" (Little did CNN know that they are helping to spread the gospel.) By allowing our own young people to be submerged in the culture, it's pulling them away from the things of God and dramatically impacting not just America but the entire world.

If you take a look at some of the headlines from chapter 1, it looks like we may have already entered the season of post-Christian America. But there is still hope, and there are still opportunities to turn this thing around.

Our Opportunity

The peak of our young generation was born in 1989, which means those kids are about 18 years old at the writing of this book. Most people come to Christ before the age of 20.[13] So there's a holy urgency that we go after this generation before they enter their 20s. Think of the implication of that last sentence. We can still capture the lion's share of this younger generation, but it's going to take the entire Church to do it, not just a really cool youth pastor, not just an effective youth volunteer. It's going to require everyone from the pastor to the deacons to the elders to the ushers to the men's ministry, the women's ministry and the seniors' ministry rallying to the cause of reaching our younger generation.

There's an opportunity right now to reach out to young people and rescue them before they get into their 20s. Think of those who are on drugs in your community, the girls who are getting pregnant, the people who walk by you in a store with tattoos and piercing, and those who are looking for a family in a gang somewhere. These are the ones who need to be rescued. The kids in your church need to be deeply engaged in the things of God and equipped to stand against the culture.

The whole church itself must be willing to change and be moldable in order to take the tried and true message of the gospel to a younger generation. God's truth never changes. But how we communicate can and should change to connect with a younger generation.

I hope you can feel the urgency in my heart. Now is the time—after two to three years of the BattleCry campaign, where we and other ministries have been banging the drum, saying, "Now is the time to focus on kids." Phase 2 has just launched, and you are a part of it by reading this book. Phase 2 is "Let's create some answers." Let's create churches into environments that really embrace young people. Let them not pass by us and our churches to find somebody in a gang or someone dealing drugs that accepts them more than we do or loves them and cares for them more than we do.

The Body of Christ has come together from many different extremes to start to focus on young people. Ministries such as those of Kay Arthur and Jack Graham (Jack is pastor of one of the largest Baptist churches in America), and people as diverse as Chuck Colson and Joyce Meyer have rallied with us to say, "We had better focus on kids right now or we're going to enter a new season in America." If all of these voices and ministry leaders can rally together, can we not as individuals rally together to rescue the kids in our own communities? Now is the time. Let's not throw up our hands and say, "Well, the world is so bad, we don't know what to do." We do know what to do, and churches are starting to do it all over America. Not just youth pastors, but entire churches are rallying together to say, "We are going to be the ones that make it really hard for teenagers to go to hell in our town."

As you read on, you will read stories of churches that are doing this. Your church can be a part, and *must* be a part. You can be key in helping ignite your church to have a heart for young people. Together, we can turn this thing around, but it's going to take every person with this book in his or her hand to take action. Read on and be inspired by others who have made a deep impact in the rescue of young people in their communities.

CREATING A CHURCH WHERE TEENS WANT *TO* COME

"Mom, do I *have* to go?" These words are commonly heard as parents coax or even bribe their kids, young and old, to get them to church each week. These parents somehow feel that if they could just get their kids to that place (the church), somehow a miracle would happen (many times it does) and they would be transformed. Unbeknownst to the young person, God has a plan to get His life injected into their heart at that particular service.

The fact is, once kids do come to Christ, we've got to make sure they're involved in a church environment that actually feeds their faith and helps them grow. They need a place that's attractive to them and that makes them *want to come back.* Too often the words we hear, "Do I really have to go?" come from kids who have committed their lives to Christ. We hear too many things like, "I love Jesus, but I just don't like the church." Why is that? We've all heard of, or have been witnesses to, fights and scandals and skirmishes among the "family of God" that cause people to become disillusioned with the church. It appears that the church is not doing in practice what they say they believe. Well, it's time for all that to change.

Out of the Storm

The culture in America and around the world is like a hurricane crashing against the hearts and minds of this young generation. Once we have young people who begin to love God and want to follow His truth, we need to make sure they have a circle of friends and relationships that help inspire their faith.

I want to plant the seed of a vision in you for the type of church that encourages this kind of growth—a vision for the kind of youth ministry and church that makes kids beat the doors down to come in. Imagine a place where young people are on fire for God. They can't wait to see their friends, hear the preacher, take notes and be challenged. They are not only absorbing, but they are also pouring what they learn into others. Imagine a place where young people come together and worship passionately with all their heart instead of just standing there through the worship service. Imagine a place where kids are so excited to be there that they actually run to the front at the beginning of the worship service so that they can be the closest to the altar as worship happens. They are either lifting their hands or they are down on their knees singing with all their heart.

Imagine a place where they step out of the middle of the hammering storm, and a culture that is trying to destroy them, when they enter church. As soon as they walk in the door they say, "Wow! I'm home. I'm on fire for God, and I feel normal being here."

Imagine a church where adults have rallied around the kids to such a degree that there is no "us and them" mentality. Young people are embraced by older people—adults, moms, dads and grandparents. All the adults welcome them to church every Sunday.

Imagine a place where kids are actually involved in the Sunday morning service as part of the worship band, as ushers, as part of the ministry team or prayer teams afterwards. Imagine a place on Sunday mornings where both the worship and preaching are not just relatable to 40- to 60-year-olds, but actually touch the hearts of 16- to 18-year-olds. They can't wait to be there, and they sit in the front row, not at the back.

What I have just described is what we are talking about: creating an environment that is a safe haven for young people's faith, where their hearts and their relationships are going to help them stay protected from the daily culture. We call these churches a NextGen church. I'm going to describe for you, in the next few chapters, examples of these churches and how your church, big or small, can become a NextGen church for your community.

Kids Know . . .

We can say that we love and care about young people, but kids know whether they are loved and accepted. We can have a youth program and a building with lights and sound for kids, but they know if the congregation considers them important. Maybe not even a word is spoken. But perhaps there is a glance from a 50-year-old as a young person walks by with an attitude, a piercing or a hairstyle that is offensive to the adults; so they look down their nose at this young person. That kid will not come back, because he or she does not feel welcome. There is no reason whatsoever for this young person to be a part of that church. The first step in becoming a NextGen church is to examine our hearts for the attitude I've just described.

Next, we can't just dump our money in the plate and say, "Here, go do youth ministry." The heart of the church must really begin to care about youth. The more we know about the brokenness that is being perpetrated on this generation, the more passionately we will care.

You must care, or you would not be reading this book. For those of us who love teenagers, it's our job *to help other people to care by putting books like this in their hands.* We must get them to watch videos and hear stories of kids who are hurting and who have really been changed by the Lord. We need to constantly parade these stories and stats to our church congregation to help people come to love and want to reach out to young people.

The first step is to rally the adults in your church around the cause of youth ministry. You can do that in a very practical way by using this book or my book *Battle Cry for a Generation*. Use the small-group discussion guide for adults that comes with each book to walk a group through six weeks of discussion to truly understand what the culture is doing to young people and what we can do in response.

Sunday Services

It's important that young people don't just "do time" when they come on Sunday morning. A lot of church services are like that. Young people are forced to go, and they sit there as if they are in prison. Wouldn't you rather see the kind of church where young people feel a connection to the senior pastor and embrace what the church stands for? Wouldn't you like to see them taking more sermon notes than the adults? It can and is happening in churches, as you will see in the next few chapters.

Overall studies show that even kids who grow up in church do not continue to attend church once they go off to college. Studies show that 88 percent do not continue in church.[1] Well, that has to change. The only way to change is to make children a part of church life while they are young, and address issues that are important to them from the Bible. We need to get young people to embrace what happens on Sunday mornings. We need to make sure that what goes on at church is feeding their souls. We need to make sure that we as pastors and preachers are speaking into *a young person's life and heart* (not speaking just to the adults).

The Sunday messages can't just be a string of platitudes to keep adults satisfied and keep the tithes coming in. I'm not suggesting that pastors need to get a piercing and wear teen fashions. But kids can tell if you love them and are paying attention to them in the way you've prepared your sermon. Whatever topic you may be preaching on, you have got to engage these young people. Throw out some nuggets for them to chew on. Give them some relatable cultural data and stories that let them know *they are part of the church!* They are not just an appendage, but a vital part of the church *now.* If we hope to keep them in church when they are older, they must be a part of the church now.

Creating a Subculture

We all live in a culture within our neighborhood and community. So far, we have examined much of the culture that is so destructive to teens and is tearing them apart. They need a safe haven where they can come in from the culture. There is a culture in any church that you can sense the moment you walk in the door. *Would teens feel more of a connection to your church and to your youth ministry than they feel to the world?* Consider that question in terms of what you know about your church.

When someone asks a young person what they're into, typical answers include favorite bands, football or other sports, music, etc. Do you think a young person ever responds, "Oh, it's my church! It's so exciting! I can't wait to go back next week. We have a great youth group. God is doing great things. I love going there; you have to come with me!" Don't get me wrong; that response could happen, and it is happening. It will happen to the kids in your church when you and others create a culture that inspires, empowers and let's young people know that in a very deep way, you are committed to them.

Take Hillsong Church as an example. The culture at large in the nation of Australia is very secular. There is not much in the way of a public Christian heritage. Yet Hillsong Church, now 20,000 to 30,000 strong, has created a subculture for young people and adults that overpowers the Godless culture at large.

When this kind of culture takes over a church, its frame of reference for life changes. The church doesn't try to compete with the world to be cool. Those who attend don't care what the culture of the world says, because they are so excited about the culture of the church that has changed their life. The ministry there continues to take place, and it keeps people coming back. It's life-giving, exciting, thrilling. It's adventurous.

It's possible to live in a very stark secular society with a thriving subculture in a church that feeds individuals to a point where the church is not only existing, but it is growing in the midst of that secular society. As a result, adults and young people are thriving in their faith and becoming more like Jesus in spite of the downward pull of the secular culture.

After visiting Hillsong Church, every person I met who was connected with the church seemed like they actually lived on a different planet from everyone else in Australia. The culture of the country had little effect on them.

Pretty Good Is Not Good Enough

All the time I hear churches and denominations say, "Oh, we have a pretty good youth ministry." The goal is not just to have a good youth group. That is not enough! We have got to have a church that rallies to the heart of a young person and organizes itself in such a way as to create a life-giving culture for young people.

I have talked with denominational leaders who have said things like, "But, Ron, we have invested $1.5 million in the young people in our denomination during the last year." That is a great statement and gesture, but if we in fact are still losing a generation, it does not matter how much we have invested in our young people. If we are still losing people, what we are doing is not quite enough.

The national youth director of the same denomination who made the statement above showed me a chart and graph depicting how their youth groups have grown during the last 5 to 10 years. He felt as if they were doing pretty good. However, after a full explanation, I charted the population growth of this generation in America for him. The growth in the overall population was much higher than the percentage of growth in his denomination's youth ministries. While he was celebrating the fact that his denomination was growing, they were actually losing ground!

We're losing market share, and the church is celebrating. According to a study by Bill Easum in 2003, although the number of churches in America has increased by 50 percent in the last century, the population has increased by 300 percent.[2] How can we celebrate when we are losing our Christian foundation in this nation?

In 1983, companies spent $100 million marketing to kids. Today, they're spending nearly $17 billion annually.[3] Shouldn't we work just as hard—if not harder—than companies such as MTV to reach out and rescue our precious young people? Young people can tell when they walk in a church building if they are valued, invested in and have been given sufficient thought to really feel like a valued member of the church community.

NextGen churches have that kind of culture. NextGen churches create a safe place out of the cultural storm where young people can thrive and take the baton of the gospel into the future. They are the kind of churches that teens *want* to get deeply involved in.

The vision we need to embrace is the dream for 100,000 churches across America and around the world to become NextGen churches. Will you embrace that vision for the sake of your children's generation? For the sake of your nation?

DREAMERS FOR GOD

And afterward, I will pour out my Spirit on all people. Your sons and daughters will prophesy, your old men will dream dreams, your young men will see visions.

JOEL 2:28

You might be thinking, *I'm not cool. I don't have any piercings or tattoos. What can I do to relate to kids? I don't want to dress like a 16-year-old.* Many of us have these same questions. So, how can we reach young people? What can we do to reach them?

Well, if you look at the executives that run MTV (you can pull them up on the Internet), you'll see that they aren't cool-looking either. They just look like executives. They're the strategists, they're the thinkers, they're the smart ones, and they're the ones plotting how they can get maximum influence and impact on as many millions of young people as they possibly can. We need to be the Christian counterparts to these secular teen strategists. We, as pastors, leaders and elders, need to be the ones who rally around the younger generation and say, "We're going to make it hard for them to go to hell. We're going to find out where they are at, what they are into, how to reach them, and where they are hanging out."

Have you ever noticed how MTV execs hire cool people to do their work on their TV programs? Our job is the same: We hire cool youth pastors and college-aged students to mentor our kids and implement the strategy we have helped design to go after these kids. It's inherent of the job of the leaders of the church to pass the baton of the gospel to the next generation. Thus, the pastor has to see himself as the chief strategist for ensuring the propagation of the gospel for future generations. Joel 2:28 is the verse we usually hear in church when we talk about reaching kids—when we think about how revival needs to come to the younger generation. We get excited anticipating when that is going to happen. Many people say, "Yes, I want my young people to be part of that revival when God really pours Himself out on the young generation."

But instead of concentrating on that part of Joel 2:28, I want to draw your attention to the "old men will dream dreams" phrase.

I used to overlook that part of the verse most of the time because I was so excited about the young people part. I thought, *I'm not going to be old for a long time yet, so I'm not going to talk or think much about the old men dreaming dreams.* But it is the older people *in our society* who dream the dreams for the younger generation, so it must be the older people *in the church* who dream dreams and engage with and care about the younger generation.

They Didn't Ask for This Garbage

When we think of the culture barrage hammering our teens, whether it's the things being sold to them, what is being written to them—movies and music—or the point-and-click pornography that's available to them, there is one thing we can all agree on: *Our children are not the ones who invented these things.*

By and large, every one of these social influences, whether it's media entertainment, technological inventions or opportunities on the Web that are destroying kids, these things were dreamed up by the older generation. In many ways, these older dreamers are preying on our young people because young people have lots of money to spend. They appeal to young people's most base desires to get them to spend their money. But the fact is, the kids didn't ask for this garbage; they were sold this garbage by people trying to make a lot of money. Of course they will tell us, "If people didn't buy it, we wouldn't make it" as if it's a moral obligation to sell people things that will destroy them just because they will buy them.

As a result, kids think, *I want my MTV.*[1] Is it really "their MTV" or is it somebody else's MTV that they find their identity in? Young people say, "I want those pants. I want that music. I want that new CD." Somebody else has made them feel important by making them feel that the company is doing something "just for them." As a result, the young people absorb and digest lyrics, values and a lifestyle that totally and completely destroy them. (Please note: They didn't ask for it; they were teased with it, and it created a desire in them to want it. It was the older generation of secular people who dreamed these perverse ideas to woo and entrap our kids.)

Once again, I ask the question: *Are we not dreamers?* Cannot we, the people who love God, dream a dream for the young people in our churches? Can we not dream a dream for the young people in our communities? Is it only the secular culture that has a dream for our youth?

Dreamers for God

In Joel 2:28, we see that the old men will dream dreams. What would it be like to have 100 kids, 500 kids, 1,000 kids in our church youth groups? What would it be like to have an incredible worship team for Wednesday night services where our kids are smitten with love for God? What would it take to have buses that pick up kids who can't find rides to church on Sunday mornings and Wednesday nights? I wonder: *If God really does want to touch and rescue this young generation, is He waiting for the older men, all the adults and the moms and the dads to dream on behalf of the young people? Where are the dreamers?* If we don't dream like that, the youth won't come.

How about you? Can you dream a dream for kids about Sunday mornings when kids can't wait to be at church, and they're dragging their friends to go with them? Can you dream a dream that you don't have to "beat" your kids over the head to invite people, because they can't wait to invite people? Where are the people who can dream big enough to encompass the young people in your entire community? Come on! We can do this together. It is going to take average people like you and me, moms and dads, business people, grandparents, to say, "I believe that God wants to do something great with the young people in this community. And I want to be a part of it."

I love the "Dream Center" concept that Tommy Barnett and his son, Matthew, came up with, and which churches are adopting around the country. It is an outreach center for people who are down and out.[2] In reality, every one of our churches ought to be *a dream center for kids*, dreaming a dream to rescue the young generation. It's not just an obligation—"I'd better do this or they are going to be lost." God *is* at work and He wants to pour out His Spirit. He is waiting for someone to step up with a dream for our youth.

The dream has got to be not just for the kids in our church but also for the kids in the community. What could such a youth center be like? What could these kids become? Young men and women going on mission trips, changing the world, influencing their schools, starting ministries, writing books and doing great things for God while they are young. We've got to rid ourselves of thinking, "Let's just try to hang on to our own" and think that we are a success when our young people are not pregnant or on drugs. What is that mentality about?! That is survival mentality. We have got to passionately dream a dream that is bigger than ourselves and passionately go after these young people! We must be consumed and mesmerized by how we can capture the heart of this generation before the world does. That is what should dominate our lives. That's what dreamers do. They are constantly brainstorming, looking for what God wants to do—and what He wants to do through them. Dreamers dream.

What If

A dreamer is someone who asks, "What if . . . ?" It is like King Saul's son, Jonathan, and his armor bearer who said, "What if God wants to deliver us?"[3] Jonathan was a dreamer. We need to be like him and ask, "*What if* God wants 1,000 kids in my church?" Maybe He wants 2,000 or 5,000. *What if* God wants to just pour out His spirit on countless young people? What would it take? What would we have to do to be ready for that as a church, as an individual, in a Sunday morning Bible study or Sunday school class? *What if* God wants to do something great on Sunday mornings with kids? What would our services have to look like? *What if* He wants to use your church to be a center for rescuing a generation? Once they come to the church, what would your church do with them? How would the church disciple them? How would the church train them to be leaders, to be disciplers of other kids? Ask what if, just *what if* God wants to do this? What would that mean, and what would all of us have to do to be ready for it and be a big part of making it happen?

It Begins with Pastors and Church Leaders

Pastors and church leaders must lead the way. I know that many thousands of pastors and church leaders have already jumped on board, as I have shared in a number of national senior pastor conferences. It has been moving to see literally hundreds of pastors weeping their eyes out as they realize they have focused on the adults and have forgotten the kids. The future of their church and the Church in America is at stake here.

Pastors, you greatly influence the hearts and minds of your entire church body. It is not just that you control purse strings; of course you do that, along with board members. I'm talking about how people see and think about what is visible. If their pastor has adopted and embraced a passion for young people, he will be continually putting the message in front of the church through video clips, announcements, bulletin blurbs or stories and testimonies. Out of sight, out of mind is what often rings true. But the more we, as pastors, put the message in front of our church members, the more their hearts will engage with the same kind of passion. It's not just about making an announcement, "Hey, we are going to be a youth-oriented church." It has to be an ongoing wooing of the congregation, and it starts with the pastor, the deacons and the leaders dreaming the dream.

This is a crisis time for *us to be the dreamers*, as we have already seen that *dreamers dominate the culture in a negative way*. A dream lures people. When you begin to act on the dream God has given you, it will entice kids to want to be part of your church. Begin with engaging the kids who are already a part of your church and get them excited about church with such an urgency that they will bring their friends. As church leaders begin to dream, then you can begin to help the congregation pick up the dream.

What could our churches be if we really became NextGen churches? Think of how many hurting, broken young people could be helped by a church that turns its heart toward its young people, as Malachi talks about.[4] The hearts of young people in your community will be turned toward you and toward Christ because you have prioritized them enough to dream on their behalf and pursue the dream to fruition.

Planning the Dream

Teen Mania Ministries offers materials to help churches dream and put a plan together to enable that dream to become a reality. It's all wrapped into the book *Revolution Youth Ministry* and a curriculum called *Double Vision*. (You can order these materials online at www.BattleCry.com.) Getting the *Double Vision* curriculum is like getting a workshop in a box. We like to say that when you spend one day in this curriculum with your leaders, you will have a 12-month plan to *double* and *disciple* your youth ministry.

The broader plan in *Double Vision* to turn around the predicament we have in America is similar to the plan that nations around the world are beginning to implement: focus on young people. As the local church, we need to begin to focus on young people like never before.

What does it mean to focus? It does not mean to just emphasize something or talk about it. It means to take action.

What kind of action? We need to reach more young people.

How many more? However many are possible.

This is the challenge we have begun to put out there. When we train youth leaders, we ask them to set a goal to *double* the size of their youth group over the course of the next 12 months and *disciple* the youth in an aggressive way to make them hardcore followers of Christ that love the Word of God. If we only *double*, then we end up with a church full of what I call "rah-rah" Christians. These people will cheer and shout at church, but they will actually live in a very ungodly way, because the Bible has not become the compass for their life. They still think the Bible is God's little "book of opinions." If they would rather not do what it says, then they won't. *Discipleship* means training them to love Jesus and His Word so much that they change the way they live to line up with what He says they should do in the Bible.

So when we say, "double and disciple," we are really intending for churches to get on board by saying, "Okay, we can do this. We can grow our youth group from 10 to 12. We can grow from 20 to 40." Not only are we emphasizing the size of the groups, but we are also training youth pastors to begin to really disciple and build strength into their young people so that they can defend their faith and communicate it in a winsome way.

ANATOMY OF A NEXTGEN CHURCH

When a church becomes a NextGen church, it will have a growing, thriving youth ministry that is doubling and discipling; but it's much more than that. It's where the entire church rallies around kids. They see that it is not just the youth pastor's job, or even the pastor's job. This has been the *mission of the church* since the beginning—to pass on the faith to an entire generation.

The Ingredients of a NextGen Church

Let's look at the essential ingredients of a NextGen church and then a number of examples of churches that are displaying this kind of urgency and productivity in reaching young people.

1. A NextGen Church Realizes the Urgency of Reaching Young People

In a NextGen church, the entire congregation understands the urgency of reaching this generation. What is at stake if we become a post-Christian nation is so huge that you as a church body have a plan to rescue as many teens as possible. All of the adults in the church have been carefully educated to understand the urgency that becomes front and center on the church's agenda. As I mentioned earlier, constantly keeping your church updated with statistics, stories and testimonies of what is going on with kids, with live testimonies or with video clips continually keeps the urgency in front of the people.

2. A NextGen Church Aggressively Plans to Grow the Youth Ministry

NextGen churches have taken on the task of not just caring about kids, but putting their care into action. If we are going to recreate the fiber of this generation, we have to do it one person at a time, one church at a time. Putting together an aggressive strategy to double your youth ministry is going to take the whole church to get involved. Yes, you have to be committed to the youth ministry enough to get enough volunteers to stand with the youth pastor. The whole church will have to stand with him—praying, caring, volunteering and giving money.

We have issued the challenge to get 100,000 churches doubling and discipling their youth groups every year for the next five years. About 3,000 churches are somewhere in that process as I write this book.[1] There are so many exciting stories of churches that are actually doing it, and we will share a few with you in the next chapter. This includes both small and large congregations. Some churches started with a youth group of 10 kids and ended up with 20 or even 50! There are churches that started to double and thought it would take a year but ended up doubling in two to three months.

The good news is that anybody can do it with the *Double Vision* workshop materials I mentioned at the end of the previous chapter. This book and curriculum is a workshop that shows youth leaders how to turn their dream for their youth ministry into a reality by planning and then executing the plan. Instead of just placating our kids by entertaining them as they "do time" in church, it's time for us to have a dream for going after these kids in our community and then put a plan together to double and disciple their number. It's a key ingredient of a NextGen church.

3. A NextGen Church Involves Everyone

Since everyone in the church feels the urgency, the next step is to constantly cast the vision and invite people in the congregation to get involved in the plan to double and disciple. Mentors are needed. People are needed to bake cookies and brownies. Drivers are needed. Small-group hosts are needed. People who will print materials and hand them out are needed. People who will love on kids and pour their life into them are needed. The men's ministries, women's ministries and senior ministries need to be involved with the dream to engage young people. There is not one ministry represented in your church that would not have a vital place in touching and rescuing a young generation. The urgency of the hour demands it.

4. A NextGen Church's Sunday Service Reflects Its Commitment to Teens

Our Sunday services must be intentional about engaging young people through the music and the message and involving them in the actual service itself—from the spirit of the adults loving on kids and putting their arms around them, to praying for them when they come forward to give their heart to Jesus. In a very real way, a kid does not have to attend that type of church for long before he or she will say, "Wait a minute, they love me! They are all about me."

This does not mean that your Sunday service becomes a youth service; but it may mean that the *adults may have to set aside some of their preferences*. Think about the 60- to 70-year-olds who would rather sing "Just as I Am" for the four hundredth Sunday in a row, but they choose to listen to a little bit more up-tempo worship in a style they don't prefer, because they have the joy of seeing young people worshiping with all their heart. They have the confidence of knowing that they are putting the baton firmly in the next generation's hand.

It's time for us as an older generation to give up preferences that we think of as "holy." A certain style is not what is holy. The Word of God is holy. The truth is holy. Making God's truth relatable to a young generation is the highest level of virtue that we could possibly live in making the gospel accessible to the next generation.

A Few Examples of NextGen Churches

Where does your church land on these four characteristics—*reaching out, growing in number, involving everyone, reflecting commitment*? As you walk down the path of becoming a NextGen church, it's important to have all four characteristics front and center in your church's priorities as you constantly monitor and build up from whatever level you are now, in each of these four areas. Now let's look at some examples of churches that are doing a great job at being a NextGen church.

Hillsong Church — Sydney, Australia

I have already mentioned that Hillsong Church in Australia is a large church. From the very beginning, they have been youth oriented. Many of you have heard of worship leader Darlene Zschech and her worship songs, including her best known "Shout to the Lord." But soon, we began to hear of the Hillsong United youth ministry, and the Hillsong United band, which became the youth group band and a phenomenon in and of itself. If you go to Hillsong on a Sunday morning, you will feel the spirit and heart of young people. You are going to feel and see lively worship that both young and old alike are rejoicing in. You are going to hear messages that young people can't wait to come back to hear more of. You are going to see a lively Friday night youth service for teens who are excited to come back on Sunday mornings. It's absolutely like revival every weekend. You will see a whole church that loves young people and can't wait to get involved in volunteering and helping with youth ministry. You are going to see older people rejoicing that young people are flooding to the front and worshiping to a rock style worship extravaganza that may not be their preference musically, but they find joy in watching the next generation fully celebrate God.[2]

As Mark Hopkins, director of Hillsong International Leadership College, recently told me, "We decided as a church that our whole church experience was going to be about reaching the next generation, not merely enjoying ourselves. So it's baked into the DNA of everything we do. Our worship, our preaching, and our programs are all focused on reaching the next generation."

Prestonwood Baptist Church — Dallas, Texas

Senior pastor Dr. Jack Graham sat down with me after I wrote *Battle Cry for a Generation*. We had lunch together to talk about the real issues confronting this youth generation. At the end of our conversation, he invited me to come back and do a BattleCry presentation for all of his 300 to 400 church staff. I came back a few months later and did a three-hour seminar on "The Status of Teenage America" and what we can do about it. I invited them to be one of the churches that double and disciple.

Dr. Graham got up after me and proclaimed that the next year, 2007, would be set aside as The Year of the Student. He wanted the entire church to rally around the student ministries. He actually pointed to the different departments represented in the room that day and said, "Those of you who are in the women's ministry, I want you to get involved in the youth ministry; and those of you involved in the seniors' ministry, you also need to find a way to engage in the student ministry." Then they had a time of prayer where all the student ministry staff came up front and all the rest of the staff prayed over them. For the entire year, they celebrated The Year of the Student. It was very visible in front of the congregation, which numbers more than 20,000 people on a regular basis. Everybody in the church knew about The Year of the Student. "We are going after young people as a church" was the constant message.

I talked to them recently about 2008; Dr. Graham proclaimed it The Year of Evangelism. Since most people come to Jesus before they are 20, it's kind of like having another year of the student. That's pretty smart of Dr. Graham, don't you think? He also has used his influence to get other pastors within his circle involved in BattleCry and the cause of reaching young people. He used his credibility and leveraged his relationships to help them catch the vision and the urgency of reaching teens now. He did this realizing it's not just about his church; it's about the Body of Christ catching the heart for rescuing this generation.[3]

New Life Church — Colorado Springs, Colorado

As you may know, New Life was the site of a shooting in December 2007. I thought it was telling that the enemy is killing our young people physically. It's also symbolic of what he is doing to young people with the cultural war we are in. I don't think it was an accident that the young people were gunned down at a church that for years has had a real focus on young people. They regularly have more than 1,500 young people in their youth group every week, and they are growing and thriving. They have set the goal to double and disciple.

At New Life, it's not just about the youth ministry being broken into small groups for discipleship, but Sunday services are very youth oriented as well. Although it is not a youth service, the youth flood to the front of the church during the worship time and are excited to be there. *They know this church is their church*, and not just for older people. They are worshiping God with excitement and love for each other. They are a family. They have a definite youth culture there and a passionate Christianity that they fully embrace and look forward to expressing corporately every week. The rest of the church rejoices in the fact that there are so many young people being affected by the church.[4]

Bethany World Outreach Center — Baton Rouge, Louisiana

Pastor Larry Stockstill has been an advocate for young people for a long time. His son, Joel, is the youth pastor. As a church, they are very focused on preaching the Word of God, but they also have very lively and passionate worship. Several years ago they decided on a small-group strategy where Joel would have 12 people that he would disciple. Then those 12 would disciple 12, and those next 12 would disciple another 12. They call it the "Principle of 12" cell-group strategy. They also decided that every fall they would focus on evangelism from September through December to get unsaved young people in the door and bring them to Christ. After that they would shut down the evangelism focus, and from January through May, they would focus on discipling all those who had been born again, making them passionate followers of Christ and getting their spiritual roots to go down deep. The summer months are spent planning the evangelism focus in the fall.

The fruit of that strategy in the last few years has been phenomenal. They now have 5,000 young people they minister to regularly in one of their groups or weekly events. This is just the young people; this does not include the adults. The adults have rallied around the passion and focus for young people in their church.[5]

Fellowship Church — Dallas, Texas

Pastor Ed Young, Jr., has done a great job at reflecting what a NextGen church could look like. Sunday mornings are very relatable to young people, from the worship band to the sermon illustrations and the creativity demonstrated. People of all ages love stories and object lessons. Pastor Young refuses to simply give principles of God's truth without having visible demonstrations on how to live out the truth. Obviously that engages young people, but it engages people of all ages too. They are very committed to youth ministry, having invested lots of money in an amazing youth center and energetic youth programs that are life-changing.[6]

The City Church — Seattle, Washington

Pastor Wendell Smith has a thriving church with campuses all over the Seattle area. His son, Judah Smith, is the youth pastor. They also have a thriving multi-site youth ministry. Almost every day of the week there are hundreds of kids meeting in different parts of the city. Once a month, or once a quarter, they all come together. When these 2,000 to 3,000 kids are together in one location, it's an explosion of celebration and excitement. They have a "deeper discipleship" program that you can enlist in if you are a young adult between18 and 20, where you are actively engaged in discipling young people in different parts of the city. The whole church rejoices in the fruit they are seeing.[7]

The Culture of NextGen Churches

There are a number of smaller churches all over the country that have decided to become NextGen churches. Read about some of the attitudes and activities they have established to make kids feel valued.

Joanie Aprill—Immanuel Fellowship in Frisco, Colorado[8]

"Growing up, my family moved frequently and switched churches even more frequently. Most of the churches we went to were focused on adults and didn't have much for the youth, and this was normal to me. The kids and teens were merely expected to behave. When I was 12, we started going to a new church that didn't seem to do things the same as the other churches I had attended. The youth were a huge part in what the church did and were valued as people and members of the church. I felt like the people—not just the pastor and youth pastor—but all of the adults cared about me. They cared about what was going on in my life and my walk with the Lord. The church was very unified as a whole. The adults valued the youth, and the youth respected the adults. I've never been in a place that was more refreshing."

Sarah Neumann—Lake Pointe Bible Church in Plymouth, Michigan[9]

"I went to a church while growing up that really made the youth group feel involved. We had a pastor who was very involved with the youth.

He would take us to Christian camps and on mission trips. Our pastor would take the first Sunday after our mission trip for us to present an overview of the trip to the rest of the church. Also, the church sometimes had the youth do skits in front of the church that supported the pastor's message. Our church was also very involved in a Bible camp, and the youth always felt encouraged to come.

"One thing that I remember is when the pastor asked me to be on the worship team, even though I was only 13 at the time! There was a bulletin board on the wall for pictures of the youth group events and a wall in the youth room where the members of the youth group would eventually get to paint their names. Our youth pastor was also very youthful and energetic. My church was always very interested and involved with the youth, and it was very encouraging."

Sarah Garnett—Zion Evangelical Lutheran Church in Worland, Wyoming[10]

"I have moved around some and have been a part of some really nice churches. The one that has impacted me the most is Zion Evangelical Lutheran Church in Worland, Wyoming. They are one of the most loving and giving churches I have ever seen. They support the youth in the church in huge ways, from sending teams to Acquire the Fire events and mission trips to being willing to lift us in prayer for anything. They have really supported the youth. They helped a girl from my church go to Bethany College of Missions in Bloomington, Minnesota. I am ever grateful for the loving church family I have in Wyoming. Even though I live in Texas now, they will always be my church family."

Grab the Vision

Becoming a NextGen church is not a far-fetched dream; some of the largest churches in the country are already doing it. Many of the smaller churches are grabbing the vision as well. It's going to take a lot of us working together, but we can do this. It is so fulfilling when your church has become a hospital for a brokenhearted generation and is full of life, passion and determination to rescue kids. If you focus on young people and show them that you love them, they will respond. They will come to Christ. When they know that they are wanted and valued, they will gladly engage deeply in becoming a member of the kingdom of God that takes the message of Christ into the future, to the whole world.

CHURCHES THAT BREAK THE MOLD: DOUBLE VISION STORIES

We have been talking about doubling and discipling the size of your youth group. As we become the dreamers for this generation, we need to dream a dream that is bigger than what the world is dreaming for them. Can you dare to imagine that your youth group could double in size? Can you imagine the same for the next year, and the next? The average youth group in America is 10 to 12 kids.[1] If you double the number for the next five years, it would be possible. Just do the math: 10 goes to 20, 20 goes to 40, 40 goes to 80, 80 goes to 160, 160 goes to 320.

I know it's hard to imagine your group increasing from 10 to 320 in just 5 short years. Don't imagine that; just imagine doubling the group from 10 to 20. What's it going to take? It is completely possible to do, because there are groups in churches of all sizes that are making plans and doubling their youth groups right now. There is no reason that you can't do the same. In a NextGen church, those kids who come in that are not Christians right now are going to find a place where they love to be and can't wait to tell their friends about.

Doubling and Discipling

Let's look at some leaders who have taken the challenge of doubling and discipling and are actually doing the deed! They're reaching kids they have never reached before, and a youth ministry that was previously going nowhere, no matter what they tried, is growing, thriving and exploding both in numbers and in spiritual depth.

Pastor Joshua Shaw: 7 to 70 in Two Years—"Emerge" Youth Group (Pennsylvania)

Pastor Joshua Shaw is an amazing youth pastor who has a heart and vision for the kids in his youth group. Pastor Josh's youth group went from 7 to 70 kids in two years. Here is Pastor Joshua Shaw's Double Vision story:

When Pastor Josh decided to pick up and move to become a youth pastor in Pennsylvania, he quickly realized that he was the new guy in town. He took over the previous youth pastor's job to whom he referred to as the "Home Town Hero." The previous youth pastor was well known in the community and grew up in the church. But some things came up in this young man's life, and he was asked to step down from his ministry position, which is where Pastor Josh came on the scene.

When Pastor Josh began, everyone thought of him as God's gift to the youth group; everyone loved him. After three months, he realized that he needed a vision and would need God's help to work with youth. He and his wife fasted for a week. Josh told me, "This was no Daniel fast; it was just water." They spent that week seeking, praying, and really seeing what was in their hearts for these kids. They came out of that week with vision and purpose.

They followed the Double Vision curriculum and began casting the vision with the church members. They sat down and looked at people's skills, then targeted those individuals to be a part of the vision and the dream God had given them for the youth group.

Pastor Josh faced much criticism and skepticism when he first rolled out the plan at a church-planning meeting with the leaders. Everyone claimed it wouldn't work and that was that. But Pastor Josh did not give up. After much internal struggle in the church, the church members got on board with the vision. Pastor Josh said that God taught him so much through this time.

They went to work on remodeling the youth room, which is now a 2,200 sq. ft. room, which increased attendance. The kids got excited and felt like they were a part of something big.

Pastor Josh's advice to fellow youth pastors is simply this. "Keep your chin down, keep focused, stay close to God and make the job you have now your dream job." He knew that God had called him to do what he was doing, and he kept going with the grace, help and love of the Lord.

Pastor Josh is continuing to disciple the youth, and his push is for attendance to be consistent and to rely on God for growth.

The next examples are direct quotes from youth ministers who have applied the Double Vision curriculum principles to their youth ministries.

Nancy Harris: 6 to 25 (Oregon)

"Going through Double Vision planning really helped us set a good foundation of leaders passionate about reaching out and mentoring the youth of this generation. The Double Vision curriculum is by far the best that we have encountered. DV gave us a step-by-step process on setting a vision, developing a dream and cultivating a plan for our youth ministry. In just 6 months we grew from only 6 teenagers to 25 and, praise God, we're still growing!"

Ben and Heidi Uitenbrobk — 24/7 Youth (Wisconsin)

"Double Vision's been so impacting on our youth ministry. The curriculum helped us put out and develop an impacting vision for our ministry! We've begun to establish, organize and develop a team of leaders to assist our youth. I love how the curriculum shows us exactly how to draw out their talents and teaches us as youth pastors to value them as they help us grow the ministry.

"As we're working on setting goals and developing our mission statement, we've implemented and defined our Core Values. We've also been focusing on Worship and just recently started our own youth worship team. We have a focus on missions and are planning to attend a Global Expeditions missions trip this summer! We've been getting the youth to be a part of the church and involved with outreaches so that when they turn 18, we don't lose them. Our prayer is that even after their time with us, they will stay actively involved in their pursuit of Christ and pour that passion into the world around them, the same way that we've poured into them."

Donald Simms
"Our deep passion to reach out to today's generation led us to Double Vision. We got the curriculum, did all the workshops and completed the workbooks. We set goals and plans with a vision that we wanted for our ministry and ran with it. We got it around October 2006, and it took until the end of the year to train all of our leaders. We started applying the principles in January 2007.

"God EXPLODED in the hearts of our young people as they became hungry and desperate for the Lord. We saw a big change in their lives; we even did a 'Back to School' event with some local youth pastors and shared with them how the curriculum helped us grow our ministry. Now, most all of them have used Double Vision and are applying it to their youth ministries. The kids were set on fire, excited about the things that God was doing—something you rarely see in many young people today.

"They were starting to get it and began to hide the Word of God in their hearts, applying it in their lives. It's a great program; the material was the best material that we've ever used, and the information is exactly what many youth ministries need. I highly recommend it to anyone who wants to grow their young people and push them closer in their relationship with the Lord!"

Alan Didio (North Carolina)
"The curriculum equipped my leadership with what they can do in order to grow as leaders. They gained vision for the youth. This curriculum

opened the leaders' hearts to be positive on what the youth can accomplish. I can say that the youth group has basically doubled since we went through the curriculum about a year ago. We went from 25 to 30 to about 60 to 70. Not only that, but we also have adult leaders who go to schools once a week and talk to teens in ISS (In-School Suspension). The multimedia resource that Teen Mania provides helps a lot and makes a difference because they are tools that a small church cannot put together alone. Also, I appreciate that Teen Mania keeps their finger on the pulse of what is going on in the world. The information helps the church remain a step ahead of the culture."

Pastor Edwin Pacheco

"In 2005, I came across the ministry of Teen Mania and BattleCry on TBN. It was the message of Ron Luce that sparked a desire to see tangible change in my ministry. He shared the frightening fact of what our youth are being faced with . . .

"Since hearing this message we, TRANSFORMED Youth Ministry, have made it our business to reach the youth of our city at any cost. We will not compromise the infallible Word of God, nor will we put any limits on who we minister to. We are living in a desperate time that should cause us to break all the existing 'religious rules' in order to reach a dying generation.

"The BattleCry Double Vision materials helped us to fully define our calling. It's been two years since we adopted the BattleCry approach to ministry, which challenges youth to engage their culture as well as youth groups to become ministries. We have done so and have seen dramatic changes. We have seen teens become fully devoted to Christ, God open doors to go into the public high schools, as well as become influential in citywide ministry . . .

"Today, our youth ministry has grown in number as well as in maturity. We are now challenged with discipling a brand-new group of over 60 young people who have just come into our ministry! We have also launched 20/20 Vision, which is an adopt-a-school initiative from the Coalition of Urban Youth Workers. Over the last year God has also opened the doors to the public schools in our community and we are currently building relationships with school officials.

"As for our efforts locally, we have made our church and community our Jerusalem. There are over 250 youth in our church. Unfortunately, not all are saved. We will not stop our work until all of them are saved, filled with the Holy Spirit, and have become advocates of their generation. We are in the plans of developing an outreach program that will minister to the homeless, the hungry, and the needy, which will be youth driven. We are also hosting leadership training for youth ministries that are based on the Double Vision resources from BattleCry.

"If you would like information about TRANSFORMED Youth Ministry and/or Bay Ridge Christian Center, please log onto www.my space.com/transformednyc."

Bruce Simms—Elev8 Youth Ministry

Bruce Simms had a heart for youth and no formal youth leadership training when his pastor asked him to lead the youth group. He faced some big obstacles right from the get-go. There was no structure to the youth group. Twenty to 25 young people were attending, but only 2 or 3 had a real passion to know God. About half the young people showed up Wednesday nights just to play games, and did not even attend the service.

"I'm the first to admit that when I started I knew nothing about youth ministry. My senior pastor heard about Teen Mania's BattleCry Leadership Summit from a letter sent by Jack Hayford," Bruce says. "I went to the Summit and saw the dynamic ministry BattleCry is doing and knew I had to bring my young people to Acquire the Fire to be a part."

At the Summit Bruce bought *Revolution YM*, the high-impact guide to youth ministry. Bruce came back with a fervor, passion and clear-cut ideas on how to Dream, Plan, and Build a purpose-filled and effective youth ministry.

Bruce was ready to change his group. He bought 100 tickets to the Anaheim Acquire the Fire event, did a highly successful fundraiser to cover the cost and had his group invite their friends. When the time for the event rolled around they took 98 teens to the event.

"This event completely, dynamically, fully changed our young people. We knew we couldn't go about doing church the same way, and we knew that there needed to be a separation, a change in how things looked and felt in the youths' minds."

Bruce brought his team back from the event ready to get serious about their ministry, even though some initial changes caused many teens to leave. In the fall of 2006, he monitored their growth from 20 to 25 people to 100 in just 3 months! In the fall of 2007, he was looking at attendance and realized they now average 200 different students a week coming to their services!

But I'm Not a Pastor; What Can I Do?

Maybe you are thinking, "But I'm not a pastor or a youth pastor; what can I do? I guess I don't have a role in all this." What you are is an *advocate*. If you have made it this far in the book, it means that you have a desire that God is stirring in your heart to do something to rescue young people.

Many of these NextGen churches started with an advocate just like you. You can become a champion for the young people in your church and in your community. Go to your youth pastor and say, "I'm here for you. I want you to know that I want to do everything I can to help your ministry to these kids and rescue this generation." It will be a huge encouragement to him or her.

I encourage you to become an advocate and think of what you can do to help your church become a NextGen church. Many of the Next-Gen churches were influenced because somebody (just a normal person like you, and not a church leader) had a heart for kids. They got a youth ministry book or other information about kids. They took it to their pastor, youth pastor and other people in the church and began to woo their hearts toward the young people. I have heard of pastors who then bought one of the books for all the deacons and elders to read. (Some have even purchased books for all the police and the teachers in their town.) They report how their church caught the vision and began to deeply engage young people. As a result, the youth ministry began to grow exponentially. All this happens because of one *advocate*. And now that advocate can be *you*!

An Advocate's Influence

Right now, think about all the people you influence or could possibly influence. How can you make this challenge personal to you? It's not Ron Luce's challenge or your youth pastor's challenge; it's yours. Think of all the people you influence at your job. Think about the people you influence in your Bible study. Think about the people you could influence by going for coffee with the pastor or some of the deacons at your church or some of the other parents of teenagers in your church or in your kids' school. Think about how you could influence the leaders in your community, whether it's the police chief or the school principal. It's amazing how one person with a passion can make a whole world of difference for kids. What about other people you know in other churches in town, and all over the country? We need an army of advocates that bang the drum all over the place, at the same time, if we are to rescue this generation!

As an advocate, the first thing to do is make a list of all the people you could influence because of your relationship with them and all the people that need to be influenced whether you know them well or not right now. Then begin to walk down that list and figure out what you can do to engage them. Next, start going down your list and acting on each item.

Find a way to get books and materials into the hands of those you want to influence.

It's one thing for you to share with people; it's another for them to be deeply informed. I encourage you to strategically place books and materials. Ask the people to read what you give them so that you can discuss the contents. Mention that you really want their opinion and thoughts on what they read. As you begin to talk to them, say, "Who else do you think should know about this?" Then you both can brainstorm people they can talk to. Make the list first and then think about what tools you want to have available to begin to influence. You may also want to invite a few friends from your church to go through the six-week small-group course that goes with *ReCreate*. This makes it so easy to watch videos and discuss together all matters concerning your role in reaching this generation.

The doubling and discipling strategy described earlier, on becoming a NextGen church, can be provoked by a committed advocate for young people who refuses to let it be easy for kids in their community to go to hell.

Remember, our job, as members of the kingdom of God, is to go after these kids *more passionately than the world is going after them*. As an advocate, you can provoke that passion and help create a culture in your church that is more powerful than the culture in the world. In this way, once a kid is committed to Christ, he finds his long-lost family—the place where he belongs, the place he can't wait to come back to. As a result, he and others like him are protected from the garbage of the world and are set up to become the champions who will influence their generation for Christ.

To get the full *RECREATE* experience, visit www.battlecry.com for videos and more information.

SECTION III

RECREATING OUR SOCIETY

We've talked about recreating the culture of our home to make it stronger than the culture of the world. We've discussed creating a church that has such a power culture that it overpowers the secular culture. A church community where kids feel safe, and their identity is found with the things of God, and not with the things of the world.

Now it's time to turn our attention to the influence we can have on the culture at large. Why should people with questionable morals and an agenda that goes in the opposite direction from biblical values be the force that shapes the culture at large? Why should they be the 2 percent that create what the 98 percent follow? Why should they be allowed to shape our whole generation without any infusion of God's truth into the national conversation? Why should their values be what dominates our culture, while there are so many good, strong believers (like you) with great values?

It's time for us to discover how we can make our voice heard and jump back into the national discussion and help change the direction our nation is headed.

DREAMERS ALWAYS WIN
(THE CULTURE WAR)

We are in a war, whether we like it or not. Our culture shapes our young people, and we must fight to get the right values into the culture and have a decent society for them to grow up in. For those who don't have parents to shield them from our present culture's heinous belief system, we must exercise our influence to protect them. We must make ourselves available to teens without parents, to teach them to see through the lies in this culture. It is a battle of ideas. It is a battle of dreams. *Whoever dreams the most compelling dream wins the culture war.* This is where we as believers must step into the national conversation of ideas.

You don't have to look far to see that most of the people who shape our culture today don't have much regard for the Bible or for the values found in the Bible. In fact, most of them who are in the 2 percent are diametrically opposed to the values in the Bible. It seems like they have done everything within their power to make commonplace the vices that are despised or looked down upon in the Bible. To accomplish this, they have built businesses without moral values for the purpose of selling stuff to kids, just for the sake of making money. Those dreams are becoming a reality.

It may not be that everyone is actually thinking, *We want to change the value system of our country*, but the media and products they make accomplish that. It may just be that the 2 percent are so interested in making money that they've decided there's no right or wrong way to do that. "Let's just make anything we can get people to buy" sounds fair enough to them.

Either way, our kids are the victims. When our kids hear a song 500 times about how to treat a woman indecently, or that the way to deal with a problem when you're mad is to shoot somebody, it has an undeniably negative effect on the listener. The current shapers of culture have successfully dreamed a dream and then wooed the lion's share of the young generation to march to the beat.

Be a Problem Solver

It's not just one person or one organization or corporation that is shaping the culture. We mentioned Viacom earlier, but there are five major communication companies that control most of the movies and music of the world. They are AOL Time Warner, Disney, Bertelsmann, News Corporation and Viacom.[1] These media empires, while in competition with each other for the majority market share, continue to drag down a young generation.

In many ways, they've won. They've won the culture war. They have dominated the culture. And they've done it by dreaming big and incorporating young people into their dream. So now it's time for us to dream.

I've encouraged you to dream a dream for your family—to recreate its culture; and to dream for your church and the kids in your community. Now, it's time to dream a dream for the culture at large.

What could we do as God-fearing citizens to help shape our culture? The task seams formidable, almost impossible. It also seems impossible to create a family culture that is stronger than the world's culture. But the fact is that we can create a culture in our family that is stronger than the world's culture if we are proactive about it.

Now we have another *seemingly impossible* task. So where do we start? We need to dream a big dream of the part of the culture we want to affect and then roll up our sleeves. We need to be smart about how we approach it. Consider Rudy Giuliani in New York City. He made some significant progress in ridding the city of pornography, but not in the way you might think. Giuliani knew that he could not use "morality" as grounds for removing them, because people would cry "freedom of speech." So he got a law passed that said there will be no porn shops within 500 feet of a school or within 1,000 feet of a place of worship. Well, there are 16,000 schools in New York City and thousands of churches and synagogues! With one signature, he shut down thousands of triple-X porn distribution centers!

We need to be *smart* about how we mean to change culture and make it better for our young people. We need to make sure that as believers we are not finger pointers. The pointed finger of condemnation is usually what the world thinks of when it thinks of Christians. So we need to come to the table with creative ideas that help bring solutions. We need to do more than preach; we need to be *problem-solvers.*

Your Dream Is Your Voice

If we want to have a voice that's able to redirect our culture and our nation, we can't just come with problems; we have to come with solutions, with creative ways of compelling young people and industry to rally around and believe that we all can make a difference.

I was contacted by the executive of a large perfume company, who had seen the cover of a *New York Times* article on this young generation.[2] The article had a picture of young people on their knees giving their hearts to Jesus. It talked about the battle that's going on with this generation, and I was interviewed about it. The executive who called me had an idea of doing a perfume that would inspire young people to be pure and not stoop to seeking to be sexy and show skin. After much research, they found that young people (not just Christians) would be *just as likely* to buy a fragrance that helped them to aspire to be pure as they would to be sexy and worldly. So we are now walking down that path together with them. Think about marketers with brands competing against each other to see who has the most virtuous fragrance! That is an example of beginning to shape culture in a major way.

We can't just say that we don't like this or we want such-and-such to be different; we've got to be the ones that dream a dream for the kids who are on drugs in our community, or the girls that are pregnant. Let's get a vision of how we can help teens deal with other issues. If we don't like them hanging out at a certain place in town, we've got to create a place for them to hang out that's wholesome and that's going to create the environment we want them to have.

People follow dreams, not directives. They won't do what they are told to do or what they are supposed to do. But they will do what they are inspired to do. Dreamers are the ones who know how to compel them to follow.

So now it's time to dream a dream for the kids you don't know, the kids who aren't in your family, the kids you may never meet. Even though you don't know all of them, they will benefit from your dream. The people who mastermind the marketing at MTV and Victoria's Secret never meet all the people they affect (so they think it doesn't really hurt anybody). They are affecting millions. They dream a dream for the sake of money and market share. But we have a more noble cause. We dream a dream on behalf of the future of our nation and the hearts of a whole generation.

PARALYZED BY THE ORDINARY

I'm afraid that too many of us find ourselves in church every week being the very embodiment of the title of this chapter. We see things that are "ordinary" and we think that's just the way it's supposed to be. Status quo is comfortable; status quo is what seems acceptable. The status quo keeps us from ruffling feathers because Christians don't want to ruffle anybody's feathers. It seems like every time we do more than the status quo, we get reprimanded by the world accusing us of being "intolerant," and so that keeps us to ourselves.

I wonder if we have been so programmed by what we call "normal American culture" that we think we're supposed to find a way to just survive in the midst of it rather then be a change agent in it?

Hypnotized by the Ordinary

We see in the passage at the end of John 21 that Peter, after having been with Jesus for three years, had seen all the miracles and heard all the parables; he was there when Jesus died and he had seen Jesus risen from the dead and ascended into heaven. Now he was pondering what he was going to do with his life. He was wondering what to do next *after he had heard the Great Commission* (see Matt. 28:18-20). His suggestion to his friends was, "I'm going fishing"; others said, "We will go with you." So in spite of all the miracles, in spite of all the life-changing encounters Peter had experienced, he still had this lingering thought of what "a normal life" was. Normal life was fishing; it's what he knew. He was going to go back to what he knew; he was going to go back to the *comfort of the known.* He was content to go back to not ruffling anybody's feathers. He was going to stay in the safe zone.

We look at the ordinary as the way things are *supposed to be.* Our equilibrium as humans is constantly geared toward, "Let's go back to what we know; let's go back to the way it used to be; let's go back to what's familiar." So, if we were familiar with or used to a culture that is constantly demeaning Christian values, that constantly parades sexualization in front of our kids, then we start to think it's normal.

Once in a while, there is a shocking interruption that we just can't believe happened, like Janet Jackson's "wardrobe malfunction" during the Super Bowl game, or Madonna and Britney Spears's kiss; but then we sort of go back to normal, even if normal gets a little bit worse. The fact is, those types of events make what is currently normal take another step down. All of a sudden, what people will accept is much lower as a whole, since it's not as bad as flashing a breast during a supposed family time of TV viewing, or watching the same-sex open-mouth kiss of two celebrities.[1]

If we get into a sort of trance with the ordinary, then that's all we'll accept. Literally, what we see is what we get. If we stay focused on what we think is normal, that becomes what we are willing to tolerate. Even though we know it is destroying our entire generation of young people, we accept it as normal. As humans, our nature is to be absorbed into the 98 percent, as followers of culture, and our decision to do so is validated by all the other people who are in the 98 percent. We think that what is all around us is adequate, so we are rendered powerless to do anything about it.

Instead of looking at what is, and allowing it to spin us into a hypnotic trance of mediocrity, we must set our eye on what could be. What is the dream that God is calling us to dream? What do we wish the teens in our community were being influenced by? Focusing on that dream will take us out of our hypnotic state of mind.

When We Legitimize the Ordinary

We often say to ourselves, "I'm an ordinary Christian. I go to church; I give money to the church; I'm a pretty good person; I don't kill anybody; I don't lie that much; I'm like everybody else, even if there are compromises in my life."

So we begin to legitimize the ordinary. Other people live like this; why would I want to be so radically different from them? Why would I lift my voice to shape a generation? Why should I have to ruffle anybody's feathers? Everybody else is kind of going downstream, so I'll go with them. We justify the compromises we make while letting the creators of this culture triumph in their quest to dominate a young generation. We legitimize our own lack of impact and view the culture we live in as not really that bad.

Jesus said that narrow is the way that leads to life, narrow is the path, but wide is the path that leads to destruction (see Matt. 7:13-14). As a result, we lose our idealism. First Corinthians 3:3 says that when we are acting worldly, we are acting like "mere men." We are not supposed to live like *mere men,* like everybody else.

As a result, the impact of our lives is minimized because we compare ourselves to the ordinary. Nobody else is saying much about it, so we don't want to rock the boat and allow ourselves to engage in change. Consequently, we don't even give birth to new ideas, because we are so concerned about being a part of the ordinary.

Break Out of the Ordinary

We have to deal with the fact that the people who are destroying our kids do so on *our watch.* They are doing so *while we watch.* They did so while *we allowed it to happen,* even if we may not have caused it. We allowed porn to come online. We didn't scream loud enough, and it became tolerated in our society.

Our impact has been minimized, because we have become addicted and mesmerized by the ordinary. If we see something happen that is horrible, we try to justify our lack of involvement. We're quick to point out the people who are putting horrible things in movies or on TV screens, *yet we do not do anything*. Doing nothing legitimizes our culture.

As believers, as followers of Christ, we must open our eyes and realize that for too long we've been in a trance, along with everybody else addicted to the ordinary. If we don't wake up, we will continue to let the wrong people shape society. They are not afraid to ruffle feathers. Most of the feathers they ruffle are moral feathers, and if we object, they call us narrow-minded prudes.

It's time for us to call them what they are: *virtue terrorists* who make money by ripping any kind of moral virtue from our young ones. We must tear ourselves away from the "trance of the ordinary" and ask what God wants us to do for our community and nation. It's time for us to rise up and not allow this to happen anymore!

It's time for us to break the stranglehold of our culture and use our voices to shape the direction of this nation for our younger generation. *What they become is what we allow them to become;* what they buy is what we *allow* to be sold in this country. What is common vernacular and what is normal culture is what we *allow* to be common vernacular and culture. It's time to wake up and see that the future of this nation and the health of this young generation are in *our hands*.

WINNING THE PR WAR

In the spring of 2006, we had one of our biggest BattleCry events of the year. We were expecting 25,000 young people from hundreds of churches to come to Giant Stadium in San Francisco, California. These young people would be coming together to pledge themselves to physical purity, to love God and do whatever it took to stand up for the moral purity of their generation.

We decided that it would be an exciting opportunity to make a difference by inviting these kids to come early to the San Francisco city hall and do a BattleCry rally there. The point of the rally was to allow them to let their voice be heard and let people know all over the nation that there are young people who love God and want to commit themselves to purity. So we got permission to use the steps in front of city hall. You may remember that several years ago, this is the same place where hundreds of homosexual couples were married in a civil ceremony by the mayor of San Francisco.

We had heard several weeks in advance that protestors were going to show up. But we weren't expecting anything like what happened.

When we arrived, there were about 300 young people there who had braved the rain to stand up for purity in their generation. We were met by about a hundred protestors (most of them were men dressed like women) who used bullhorns to shout horrible things at these young people. They screamed things like, "We don't want to marry you, we just want to _____ you." They had taken hymns and other Christian songs and put perverted lyrics to them and sang them as loud as they could.

You would have been so proud of our young people. Their response was just to pray and be kind and loving, while singing worship songs. The media, of course, showed up because they love a catfight. But they saw how these kids were so loving and how the very people who were protesting and saying, "This is a mean-spirited Christianity thing" were the ones who were yelling and angry.

It was shocking to see how violently opposed the protestors were to young people who just wanted to stand up for purity. As I reflect on it, I wonder why it is that the ultra-liberal people in San Francisco were so tolerant of every other group except Christians. It dawned on me that they don't mind if we keep our Christianity in our little youth group or in our church basement, as long as it stays inside four walls. But they really don't want us to bring it out into the public sector; they don't want us to bring it to the city hall or to the front steps of the courthouse. They don't want us to bring it up in politics or in the discussion of the values of our nation. Why? Because *they have virtually dominated our thinking and culture unopposed for many years*. It angers them to see someone make a visible stand, saying, "We don't like this; we want the nation to go a different direction." They know that a person's verbalized beliefs can have a great impact. Voicing beliefs can change culture, shape opinion and change policy.

Their anger was a sign to me that we were doing something right. We had put our finger on a hornet's nest by accident. Instead of being brought to silence, it made me want to encourage the teens to express their faith all the more.

Two months later, when we arrived in Philadelphia for an event, we had 138 groups all over America doing BattleCry rallies at their city halls or on the courthouse steps. Once these young people all over the country saw what had happened in San Francisco, it rallied them to take a stand in their own regions. Here are some headlines and excerpts from news articles reporting on these rallies:

- Lansing, MI: "Local Teens Rally for Their Generation." Local Christian teens will pray, sing and hope for their generation's future today at the Capitol . . .[1]

- Cape Girardeau, MO: "Teens in Cape Girardeau Protest Sex and Violence in Media." Approximately 30 members of local church groups demonstrated in front of Cape Girardeau City Hall on Friday in what they're calling a "battle cry" for a reclamation of Christian values among teens . . .[2]

- Michigan City, IN: "Church Protests Sex, Violence in Media." Internet pornography and MTV were specific targets . . .[3]

- Detroit, MI: "Teens Spurn Negative Values, Farmington Group's Rally Decries Drink, Drugs, Sex." They stood under dark, drizzling skies to take a stand Friday afternoon against sex, drugs and MTV. A group of seven teens—ages 14 through 17, who are members of St. Gerald Catholic Church—carried rosaries and held picket signs, with messages such as, "Sex Doesn't Sell Me" and "MTV" beneath a red slashed circle . . .[4]

- Midland, TX: "Teens Seeking Morality Gather for 'BattleCry.'" Today in front of the Midland County Courthouse local teens will gather for a "BattleCry Youth Rally and Press Conference" to sound a call encouraging Christian youth to fight back against a pervasive popular culture they say promotes sex, violence, drugs and immorality . . .[5]

- Philadelphia, PA: "Teen Crusade: Tune Out, Not In, A Christian Group Comes to Town with a Message on Pop Culture." Thousands of teens are rallying at the Wachovia Spectrum this weekend to sound a battle cry against pop culture . . .[6]

- San Francisco, CA: "Not Welcome in San Francisco." The group, called "BattleCry for a Generation," uses the Bible to counter what it calls corrupting influences in the media. But the *San Francisco Chronicle* reports that about 50 counter-protesters denounced the gathering as a "fascist mega-pep rally . . ." [7]

This is our opportunity as Christians to jump in the middle and say, "Wait a minute; we want to have a voice in the direction of our country as well!"

The PR War

We received lots of secular media coverage as a result of the BattleCry event in San Francisco. In fact, when we returned the next year, in spring 2007, we had even more secular coverage and more protestors. CNN, ABC, Fox News and many other news outlets televised what was about to happen. (Go to www.battlecry.com to see *Night Line* and CNN clips.) We found that, because of all the news coverage showing the violent response of the protesters to the kids, the perception conveyed by the media was that the event was a "mean-spirited, battle-oriented kind of ministry." The media's predisposition toward favoring the secular culture over Christianity got them to interview people who were yelling things like, "These Christians are angry!" when in fact it was the protesters who were angry. (The media allowed a random protestor on the street to describe what kind of Christians we are? How can that be unbiased reporting?!) In actuality, the teens were so loving and kind that they did not get equal media time. We started hearing things like, "Why do these people always have to talk about battle all the time? And why are they so mean?" when in fact, we weren't mean at all.

It is exactly this kind of reporting that continues to reinforce the misperception of mean-spiritedness about followers of Christ. The secular culture of our country has succeeded in establishing a dominant negative perception of Christianity. And it's true that the character portrayals in movies and television programs portray Christians in a very negative light. A recent book, titled *unChristian,* documents six of the main trends that non-Christians feel about Christianity. They think all Christians are:

1. Hypocritical
2. Too focused on getting converts
3. Anti-homosexual
4. Sheltered
5. Too political
6. Judgmental[8]

While it may be true that some Christians have given people reason to believe these things, most believers are not like this. It's just that the PR war has been won by those of a different belief system, and they have succeeded in creating a negative perception of everything Christian. To the mass population, perception is reality. Hence, we must over-communicate with the love of Christ to overcome the bias against Christianity in our culture.

As we meet people who are not Christians, or people who are shaping the culture, we've got to overwhelm them with God's love. As we talk about any of these issues, we need to talk about love. In fact, we need to display the kind of love and warmth that's real and genuine, and not just focus on debating ideas. We are battling for the hearts and souls of people, no matter what persuasion they might be.

How Is Secular Culture Influenced?

There are four major ways that culture is influenced:

1. Entertainment, sports
2. Education

3. Government and law

4. Business

Years ago, any number of groups began to infiltrate different levels of society, from women's rights movement to equality for almost any cause or sector of people you can imagine. For example, the homosexual agenda has very cleverly used tactics to invade each of these four areas. There is a distinct plan that focused on changing the perception of homosexuality in this country.[9] This plan was created in 1972 by the National Coalition of Gay organizations.[10]

Entertainment

With the onset of AIDS, there was a huge PR problem for the homosexual community and they would have been accused of causing the "bubonic plague" of America. So they began to aggressively invade each of the areas. It began in entertainment. They began enlisting as many programs as they could. Below I have included a list of some very familiar shows with homosexual characters. The first homosexual character shown on public television was in the 1970s. Now there's almost one homosexual character in every program. There are 369 homosexual characters that regularly appear on our television screens today, to be exact. Now they entertain us; we laugh with them and at homosexual jokes. Homosexuality has been normalized into the culture of our entertainment.

Some familiar television shows that include or have included regular homosexual characters:

- *All in the Family* (sitcom) CBS 1971-1979
- *All My Children* (serial daytime drama) ABC 1970-present
- *As the World Turns* (daytime serial drama) CBS 1956-present
- *The Kids in the Hall* (sketch comedy) CBC 1989-1995

- *Roseanne* (sitcom) ABC 1988-1997
- *The Simpsons* (animated sitcom) FOX 1989-present
- *One Life to Live* (serial daytime drama) ABC 1968-present
- *The Real World* (video-verité documentary) MTV 1992-present
- *Beverly Hills 90210* (high school/college drama) FOX 1990-2000
- *General Hospital* (daytime serial drama) ABC 1963-present
- *Friends* (sitcom) NBC 1994-2004
- *Nash Bridges* (police drama) CBS 1996-2001
- *ER* (medical drama) NBC 1994-present
- *Will & Grace* (sitcom) NBC 1998-2006
- *Sex and the City* (sitcom) HBO 1998-2004
- *Felicity* (teen angst drama) WB 1998-2002
- *Dawson's Creek* (teen angst drama) WB 1998-2003
- *Survivor* ("reality" contest) CBS 2000-present
- *Big Brother* ("reality" contest) CBS 2000-present
- *Undressed* (anthology serial drama/comedy) MTV 1999-2002
- *Six Feet Under* (drama) HBO 2001-2005
- *Spyder Games* (serial drama) MTV 2001
- *Boston Public* (high school drama) Fox 2000-2005
- *The Sopranos* (mafia drama) HBO 1999-2007
- *Amazing Race* (long format game show) CBS 2001-present
- *The Real World* (video-verité documentary) MTV 1992-present
- *The Shield* (police drama) FX 2002-present
- *Degrassi: The Next Generation* (teen drama) CTV and The N 2001-present
- *The Wire* (crime/police drama) HBO 2002-present
- *Reno 911!* (sitcom) Comedy Central 2003-present
- *The O.C.* (drama) Fox 2003-2007
- *Queer Eye for the Straight Guy* (make-over) Bravo [USA] 2003-2007
- *The L Word* (drama) Showtime 2004-present
- *Passions* (daytime serial drama) NBC 1999-2007, DirecTV 2007-2008

- *Rescue Me* (drama) FX 2004-present
- *Drawn Together* (animated sitcom) Comedy Central 2004-present
- *Nip/Tuck* (medical drama) FX 2003-present
- *Desperate Housewives* (drama-comedy) ABC 2004-present
- *Veronica Mars* (drama/mystery) UPN 2004-2006, CW 2006-present
- *Everwood* (drama) WB 2002-2006
- *Doctor Who* (science fiction drama) BBC 1963-1989, 2005-present
- *The Office* (sitcom) NBC 2005-present
- *Commander In Chief* (drama) ABC 2005-2006
- *Law & Order* (crime drama) NBC 1990-present
- *General Hospital* (serial drama) ABC 1963-present
- *As the World Turns* (serial drama) CBS 1956-present
- *Love Monkey* (drama) CBS 2006, VH1 2006
- *So NoTORIous* (comedy) VH-1 2006-present
- *Project Runway* (contest) Bravo [USA] 2004-present
- *American Dad* (animated sitcom) Fox 2005-present
- *All My Children* (serial daytime drama) ABC 1970-present
- *The View* (talk show) ABC 1997-present
- *Ugly Betty* (comedy/drama) ABC 2006-present
- *Dirt* (drama) FX 2007-present
- *Greek* (college drama/comedy) ABC Family 2007
- *Sophie* (sitcom) CBC 2008-present
- PrideVision Homosexual Network, 6 shows airing between 2001-2003
- OutTV Homosexual Network, 5 shows airing between 2001-present[11]

Education

In the realm of education, there are continual attempts to get laws passed in a number of different places. One such law was recently passed in California. It was a bill passed to forbid the use of the words "mom" and "dad" in a textbook because it might make people who come from a same-sex home feel a little bit bad.[12]

Children have the opportunity to read books like *Asha's Mums*. This book tells the simple story of a school field trip. Asha takes the permission form home to get signed by her two moms. She returns to school the next day and her teacher tells her that she can't have two moms. A friend then sticks up for her and says you can have two moms just like you have two aunts or two daddies or two grandmas.[13]

Headway has been made in a number of different states regarding equal rights for people who are homosexual couples.

As believers, we don't hate people and we don't condone any crime toward anyone. Our focus should never be to point the finger of condemnation at anyone. Every heart needs Christ, and every person is empty until he or she comes to Christ, no matter what sin (even if they don't think it is a sin). Our job is not to convince people of their sin; we will never win that argument. Our job is to help people discover that they are empty and broken without Jesus in the center of their life!

I only point out what they (when I say "they," I mean a small group of activists who are bent on shaping the rest of our culture) are doing so that we can know the designs they have on our children. Even things like homosexual adoption of children, where 65,000 children are being raised by same-sex "parents," is an attempt to normalize the homosexual lifestyle.[14] The argument is made that as long as it is a loving home, why should they not be able to adopt? Children raised by same-sex parents are now on video (as you can see on YouTube) asking politicians for homosexual marriage to be legalized. Doing this gets the kids to convince their peers that homosexual parenthood is really just another model of a "normal family."[15]

It's all part of an attempt to normalize the homosexual lifestyle in this culture. Much of the PR about homosexuality says that *people can't help it; they're just born that way*. But the fact is that there's no biological proof that shows people are just born that way. Yet if that position is presented enough times, even Christians begin to sympathize with the plight of "being persecuted" for no reason. I think we should sympa-thize with homosexuals because they are hurting and confused, but not for the reasons the activists espouse.

As a result of all of this, some teenagers are genuinely confused about their sexual identity. Today, it's not uncommon for teens to ex-periment with same-sex kissing and dating. It's not enough for us as parents or the older generation just to be mad at their behavior. What we should be mad at is that we have allowed this kind of influence to just go unfettered in the media and even in textbooks in our schools. We need to have a heart of compassion for these kids who, because of the suggestion culture has made that "maybe they were born this way," now really are confused. Instead of violently responding in anger to-ward teenagers who struggle with this issue, we need to respond in compassion with clarity.

For example, I recently received an email from a young man we will call Bryan. He said that he had been coming to our Acquire the Fire youth events for years. When he was 15 years old, he felt he was strug-gling with his sexual identity. His mom came up to him one day and asked, "Son, are you a homosexual?" He said, "Well, as a matter of fact, I have been struggling with thoughts about that." She got mad, blew up, and walked out of the room. Then she proceeded to tell her hus-band, his stepdad, about the whole thing. The stepdad got so angry with this young man that he threw him out of the house. Please note that this mom and stepdad are church-going people.

This young man then began to go from home to home, living in dif-ferent foster care places. He turned to a full-blown homosexual lifestyle, which in his case involved drugs and drinking. After 7 years of living that lifestyle, he finally came back to the Lord. Think how much of that could have been prevented if, in a loving way, these parents understood that young people are being shaped and confused by the garbage being crammed down their throats.

The fact is, if we find the kids in our home or the kids in our neighborhood confused about their sexual identity, we need to reach out to them in compassion and show them that their identity is far beyond their sexual orientation. They need to look solely in who God made them to be. Their sexuality is only one part of their identity. There are many tools out there to help us know how to deal with these issues with our kids, including ministries like Exodus International.

Again, let me emphasize, there is *no* good reason to persecute anyone for a sin if they are not believers. Would you get mad at a dog for barking? A sinner sins naturally. The issue is their heart, not the thing they are doing. But their tactic of continuing to say, "We were born that way," seems to be working, as many young people raised in church truly believe this line of reasoning.

Business

Then, of course, there is business. There are many businesses owned by homosexual activists who make lots of money and are able to promote their cause. They've also convinced businesses to advertise in their TV programs and magazines. They threaten public companies that if they are really going to be equality driven, they have to support their initiatives too. They accuse people of being bigoted and of not being open-minded if they are not given spousal rights and medical coverage for same-sex couples.

So you can see the reason they have made progress; *they've had a plan and they are organized around it.* Our kids are being shaped by their plan. Those who espouse the homosexual agenda are smart. They are methodical. The point here, however, is not only to point out homosexual activism, but to ask, *What is our plan?*

Muslim Agenda

In spite of the fact that our television screens are being filled with news of Muslim terrorism almost nightly, there has been a concerted effort to normalize Islam in our nation from as early as the 1960s and 1970s. Already in America, there are schools openly teaching students about Islam.[16] In fact, when I recently met a leading ministry leader in Uganda, he described to me the strategy mapped out years ago by Saudi Arabia. They had planned to bring some of the brightest people in African Muslim nations to America for education so that they could be on the front lines to advance their cause. Many of those Muslims are still here doing just that.

The Islamic Brotherhood continues to increase in number in the United States. These individuals openly stand against radical, violent Islamic groups, yet they overtly promote their opinion on the separation of religion and politics. They believe that there can't be any such separation and look forward to the day when the majority of Americans support their law.[17]

Dr. Anis Shorrosh, author of *Islam Revealed*, wrote a doctoral dissertation on how to make the United States a Muslim nation within 20 years.[18] This man is solely responsible for starting more mosques in America than any other person. In addition, Muslims have aggressive agendas in many different nations, including Cambodia, where there has been a rapid growth of schools and mosques.[19] All of this points to the fact that Islam has become a viable force in our culture, even though right now members of the Islamic faith comprise only .5 percent of the U.S. population.[20]

WHO TOLD US TO SHUT UP?

Why is it that believers feel so inhibited to let themselves be heard? Where do we get the idea that it's okay for everybody else to voice their values in demonstrative ways, yet believers somehow are not worthy? Why do we think our ideas don't have a right to be at the table of ideas in our land?

From the very beginning, Christianity has been a very vocal and public expression. In the Early Church, when people committed their lives to Christ, they confessed their belief in Christ in front of the masses and, as a result, many were killed in stadiums for it. Most of the apostles and many of the believers in the days of the Roman rule were killed in the arena because of confessing their faith in a very public way. By refusing to bow their knee to the emperor, who was thought of as a god, these Christians paid the ultimate price.[1]

The reason Christianity spread is because the natural expression of somebody who finds God is, "I've got to tell somebody!" A person who has the cure for cancer would not keep it to himself. When you know the answer to life itself, the natural expression is, "I've got to tell someone." In the first century, people like Paul, Barnabas and Silas traveled to and fro over the known world to share the good news.[2] Missionaries have gone to perilous places all over Africa, into disease-ridden continents and nations, knowing that they would probably lose there lives while sharing the good news of Jesus Christ. They went anyway, because the message was so compelling that they had to voice it.

In fact, much of the art renaissance that happened all across Europe in the 1500s was an expression of the artists' faith in Christ. When you look at masterpieces that Michelangelo[3] produced and the amazing works of music that Handel[4] composed, you can see that these people weren't shy and inhibited, afraid to express themselves. These were people who had the outflow of what was on the inside of them shaping their artwork for all to see.

Shaping the Culture

From the very beginning, not only was Christianity expressive and vocal, but it had a big part of shaping culture. What part of Europe hasn't been shaped by the great painters and artists who sculpted marble, built buildings, painted magnificent canvases and composed music all to the glory of God?

Think of the shapers of the Constitution of the United States and the Founding Fathers as they expressed their faith in many of the founding documents of the United States of America. Their Christian beliefs were indeed a part of their life and expressed through everything they did.

Now fast-forward to the twenty-first century in the United States, where somehow the message has been received: *Everyone has the freedom to express his or her belief system and values, except if you're a Christian.* Somehow, if you express your Christianity, you are less than tolerant and you don't care about other people.

Yet horrible things are being displayed in events like "gay pride days" down the center of our streets, all across America. (Many of these events show men in little to no clothing, kissing and fondling each other as they march.[5]) The vile and crude expressions of "freedom of speech" are never condemned as less than tolerant.

Atrocities are being displayed for all to see in the sex education programs in our classrooms across America. Much of this happens without parental consent because somehow somebody *felt that it was the right thing to educate kids in ways that parents never approved.* Proponents of teaching that we would not approve obtained seats on the school boards and have opened up our children's minds to the crudest practices imaginable. (Consider a Maine school system that passes out condoms to 11-year-olds.)[6]

We've been told, in no uncertain terms, that we are to be seen and not heard as Christians. We have been given the not so subtle message that "What you believe is erroneous, and you really have no right for public discourse of your ideas." Too many of those who would call themselves followers of Christ have bought that message and internalized it. They have indeed found themselves judging other Christians who are vocal: "Well, we are just supposed to be loving, and loving means never saying anything." That line of thought is the very reason that secular beliefs have begun to dominate our culture.

In the culture war, whoever speaks up the most gets to shape the culture. If we don't speak up, we lose. We speak with our vote, with our creativity, with our noticing when there are hints of unbiblical values being displayed in our communities.

Many nations around the world think of America as a "Christian nation" because we imprint "In God we trust" on our money. But when they look at us, they find the crudest music, videos, television and movies that anyone could possibly create. As long as secularists are successful in telling us to shut our mouths, they will rule the land. They will make us feel like we are being judgmental anytime we want to express our faith and have a voice. As long as we stay silent, they will continue to dominate our culture and take this next young generation to a death of plundered morality that would be truly unthinkable to our forefathers.

A Voice that Engages the Heart

As we speak up, we need to be careful to speak kindly, and without condemnation. We need to have a voice of compassion, not of anger.

We don't finger-point and call people sinners, but we do demonstrate our love in creative ways.

Our voice needs to sound like the voice of Christ as we communicate our ideals, values and faith. We need to step out of a defensive position and get offensive in terms of creatively engaging people in deep thought so that they at least have to consider what we say instead of simply dismissing us. Is this not what Jesus did with His parables, stories and object lessons? He made people think through the issues of life, with faith and the Creator God as a backdrop. They had to wrestle with their faith and their own connection to God, based on the stories He told.

We need to do the same thing through the arts, through our churches, through our sermons, through our billboards. Well, you get the point. It's called taking our culture back! It's realizing that those who have told us that we are to be seen and not heard are the ones lifting their voices and shaping this young generation. In reality, *God wants us to be seen and heard.* We cannot try to engage the matters of the heart from a cerebral perspective only; our voices must be loving, creative and potent so that the message goes to the heart.

MAKING CREATIVE NOISE

Do you feel the freedom to let your voice be heard? Have you been inspired to dream a dream to make a difference for young people in your home and in your community, in your world and the nation? Please don't go out and start with a banner or bullhorn. Creative noise has to be expressed with art, the expression of our faith. It starts out with a dream. What is the area in which you feel most compelled to rescue kids?

Creative Noises in Our Culture

First of all, responding to the world is one of the ways that we can communicate our values even though it is a more defensive posture. When we see things that go against what we hold to be true values and lifestyle, we need to say something. We can be kind about it, but we can make some noise. For example, if you see billboards that are perverse, don't allow the images to stay there. What we allow is what becomes normal. What we allow is what the standard becomes. If you see commercials on your television set that upset you, and you know that you would not want your kids to see them, or other people's kids to see them, make a stand. Say to the television station, "We don't appreciate this programming." Tell your friends at church, "Hey, let's tell these guys that we don't want this garbage." You not only protect your kids, but you also protect the kids all over the community. When you see these massive billboards in a mall that are showing women with hardly any clothes on, you take a stand and find out how you can get those images taken down. You don't just protect your eyes; you protect your family's eyes and the eyes of the entire community.

Think about the things you hear on the radio, the things you see on MTV, the things you hear in common speech. Whether it's schools that are teaching a certain lifestyle, or schools that permit birth control to be dispersed on campus, any and every time we see the values of the Bible trampled, we ought to stand up and say, "Wait a minute; do we really want our children around that? Do we really want them to see these commercials? Do we really want this kind of community?" Even non-Christians, when you appeal to their need to protect the children in their community, many times they want to do the right thing too.

Your Creative Noise in the Culture

We all need to have a defensive side, but more important is the need to creatively think about how we can use our voices to influence the people of all ages in our town. Think about all the different ways that you could get them involved, especially with Internet access that gives us so many opportunities to take what used to be a small voice and broadcast it to the world. Blogging is just one of the many ways you can do this. You can choose to start a blog and get people to subscribe to it so that the word spreads virtually around the Internet on issues that you may want people to engage and gather momentum for the purpose of social change.

A Video Post

With the advent of YouTube and GodTube and other Internet sites, you can make videos that are seen worldwide by hundreds of thousands, even millions, of people. Just a few short years ago, this would have been virtually impossible without millions of dollars. Maybe you know how to do video, or your kids do, or you know someone in your neighborhood who will join with you to regularly post videos and send out the link to an email list.

Writing

Whether it's writing poems or stories, you may have a creative gift to express yourself. There are a number of websites that will let you and your teen post your writing. One popular site for young writers is www.poetry.com. For the artists, check out www.deviantart.com. Neither of these sites is specifically for Christians and can be used as a tool to share your faith. Other options to check out include the Christian Writers guild at www.christianwritersguild.com. Personal Web pages and blogs are other great ways to express written thoughts.

Music

Maybe you are talented in music or know some young people who are talented in music. Stand up and help them express their voice and use their talent by standing behind them financially so that they can get the word out to their generation.

I want to encourage you to begin to look for young people in your church or community who may have a gift for music. You might not be musically inclined, but you can still stand behind them. You can help them buy gear if they need equipment. You can find ways to help them make a demo record and actually get it to a record company. They might even get a record deal out of it. You can help them find local venues or fund their travel. You might also be able to give them platforms to express their gift. A friend of mine, Pat Fleming, took a young band of teenagers underneath his wing to both mentor them spiritually and invest in them financially. He helped fund their dream to minister and reach their generation through their gifting.

The fact is that secular kids have people all the time who believe in them and step up to the plate with money to help them live their dream.

We are going to have to do the same if we want God-fearing people to have more influence in our nation.

Board of Education

Another way to use your voice is to get involved in the local school system. You may not realize it, but as a member of the local school board, you have tremendous opportunity to influence what is allowed in the schools—particularly in their libraries and curriculum. Find out when the elections are. Find out when people get nominated. Find out the process of getting elected. Watch it for a few years and see how you can get involved. We want there to be Christian people with biblical morals and values involved in making the decisions about sex education and whether or not condoms should be passed out in the schools to 11-year-olds. You can end up being the stop cap by preventing rude and crude teachings and videos from getting into schools. Not only do you protect your kids, but you also protect everyone else's kids as well.

Government

Think about how you can get involved in running for office. This might be for your local city council or even for mayor. Remember that getting involved in the government is one way that you can help shape the culture.

Just like when our country began, everyone can benefit from a wholesome and decent culture. However, that is only going to happen if concerned people jump into the fray of shaping this world. Sure, it's a risk. Sure, it's uncomfortable. Sure, it may not be what you thought you would do. But it's going to take a willingness to sacrifice in order to shape the culture and protect the kids who don't have godly Christian parents.

Our Real Job

Our job is to make sure that the fervent passion for God, the standard of the kind of lives we want to live, and the kind of culture that we want to have are clearly and viably expressed in a way that shapes our culture in a positive manner. We need to clearly communicate our values in a way that makes creative noise in our culture. We must engage the entertainment world by supporting good entertainment such as *The Chronicles of Narnia* series or by making noise against some of the destructive entertainment. We need to engage in government by standing up for godly, wholesome government leaders or by entering the political arena ourselves. We need to participate in education by making noise about the horrible things that are sneaking into our education system and by standing up for wholesome teaching such as teaching abstinence in sex education. We need to stand behind businesses that represent moral values, such as Hobby Lobby and Chick-fil-A, and let our voice be heard. Remember, if we are business owners, we have opportunity to support wholesome causes in our community. We have all heard the announcer at a ball game or concert say, "It's time to make some noise!" Well, this is the word to the Body of Christ: "It's time to make some noise!" Let's do it with all our hearts in a creative way that compels people to listen.

TEENS WHO ARE CHANGING THEIR GENERATION

As I travel around the country speaking to hundreds of thousands of teenagers each year, it's exciting to see that young people are beginning to jump into the middle of the fight to take their generation back. I have heard some very inspirational stories of young people who have not just sat back and let the culture destroy their peers. I hope these stories inspire you, excite you, thrill you and compel you to action.

Morality at the Mall

Victoria's Secret was doing what they thought was just another day of business when a group of 30 teenagers decided to talk some sense into their local Victoria's Secret store at the mall. Standing outside the store, the first student went in and asked for the manager. The manager came to see him, and the student asked, "Sir, would you please take down these posters? They are not good for our generation; they are not good for the guys to see; they make us look at women in all the wrong ways; it doesn't really give women dignity like they deserve." The manager got mad and kicked him out.

So the second member of the youth group went in asked to see the manager. The manager came and the next student said, "Sir, would you please take down your posters? They are destroying our generation, destroying how we look at women." The manager got mad and kicked him out. So, they sent in number three. He, too, asked to see the manager, and the same scenario happened. All 30 members in the youth group made it in, one at a time.

Finally, after the manager had kicked out the last student, the whole youth group went in and pleaded, "Sir, would you please take down the posters? Don't you know that they are destroying our generation? Don't you care about what you are doing to us?" The whole store got completely silent and the shoppers froze as they listened to these students. The manager carefully, intentionally walked over and began to take down the posters.

Now, that is an example of young people who had an idea and a creative way to impact the culture. What they did was not about just protecting themselves, it was about protecting every kid in their community from having to be exposed to the garbage that Victoria's Secret puts in their shop windows.

Moving Product Off the Shelf

During Christmas, a youth group from Arizona found out about a store that was selling what they called "pornaments." These ornaments were actually pornography. We at Teen Mania found out about it and emailed our massive list of young people around the country to find out if they would do something about these sorts of items being sold during Christmas. Kids started going into stores with little video cameras and confronted the sales people, asking them, "Is there nothing sacred? Not even Christmas anymore?" Some salespeople walked off the job and quit. Other managers decided to pull the "pornaments" off the shelves right then. But then the youth group decided to get smarter and engage the maker of these items that were being sold in stores all across the state of Arizona. The youth group wrote a letter asking the company to cease from selling. The company did pull the item from their inventory, just because one youth group took action.[1]

Crusader Against Slavery

Zack Hunter is another young man who at 15 years old began to crusade across the country to stop slavery as we know it. When he was 12, he started reading books about slavery that led him to discover that there are 27 million slaves today.[2] He went on to start an organization called Loose Change to Loosen Chains to encourage young people and adults to raise support for anti-slavery organizations such as IMJ, Free the Slaves, Child Voice International, Rug Mark and Justice for Children International. Today, Zack is the global youth spokesperson for Walden Media's Amazing Change campaign and the author of *Be the Change: Your Guide to Freeing Slaves and Changing the World in 45 Days While Still Going to School*.[3] As Zach himself says, "We need to raise money to do this. We need to stop international slavery and slavery around the world where people by the millions are still enslaved by oppressive regimes."

Teen Becomes Mayor

At 16 years old, Michael Sessions decided to run for mayor in his town in Michigan. He got all of his friends out campaigning, even though they were not old enough to vote. At first people thought of it as a joke, but on election day, Michael actually won the position of mayor in his town. Michael spent half of his days during his senior year of high school in school and took care of his responsibilities as mayor for the remaining half (in his town, being mayor was only a part-time job).[4]

Revolution on Campus

Before Jordan Kintner came to the Honor Academy during his senior year, God created a revolution in Jordan's heart that caused a revolution at his school. It was nearly the end of his senior year, and he was desperate to make an impact on his school. While God had previously used him and others from his youth group to start a prayer meeting on campus, Jordan was still not satisfied. So one day as he sat in class, he prayed, "God, if You could use me to touch this school for You, do it. Help me, Father, to make an impact on my class for You that will be remembered."

Only a few minutes after he prayed this prayer, a girl from the student body government came up and asked him if he would speak at his class' Baccalaureate service, which would be held during the same week as graduation. Jordan's heart jumped when the girl told him that he could speak on any religious topic.

A few months later, the Baccalaureate service arrived. During the presentation, Jordan told the entire group of 150 to 200 people in attendance that only a relationship with Jesus Christ would satisfy the longings of their hearts. He pleaded with those present to come and talk with him and asked them to not let his words just be a message, but to let it change their lives.

Jordan states, "This is something that I did in my teenage life that I suppose you could call 'dramatic' for God, but in all honesty I don't see it that way. I was just trying to make a difference in my school."[5]

Jesus Cookies

Brianna Keleher is another teen who is making a difference. In September 2006, Brianna went to an Acquire the Fire event held in Amherst, Massachusetts. At one point during the session, a Compassion International advertisement came on that immediately grabbed her attention. When the opportunity came, Brianna went over to the Compassion International booth, and in a short while she was the proud sponsor of a child in Lima, Peru.

Brianna knew that there were a lot of students at her school who also wanted to help but who wouldn't take the step of sponsoring a child for themselves. So she came up with an idea to sell "Jesus Cookies" in her class, with all of the proceeds going toward Compassion International. In three days, Brianna started selling the cookies, and from the beginning of October until the beginning of June, she was known as the "Cookie Lady." The Jesus cookies were made by kids, bought by kids, and the proceeds went to a kid. Brianna found that selling the cookies also gave her a great opportunity to talk with students about what Compassion International stands for. Today, she is still known as the Cookie Lady at her school.[6]

ON THE OTHER SIDE OF YOUR DREAM

"I will pour out my Spirit . . . [and] your sons and daughters will prophesy . . ." We've read this Scripture from Joel 2 several times. So my question to every reader is, "Who are the sons and daughters? Are they just the ones in your home? Are they just the ones that you have actually raised, or do they go beyond that?" I would encourage you to think that your sons and daughters are the sons and daughters of America; the ones we have been talking about throughout entire book; the ones that are being tantalized and crushed by those who would make a profit from their destruction. These are the sons and daughters of America and the sons and daughters of the world. Our responsibility goes beyond those who live in our home to those who are living in the culture that we are allowing to flourish.

We have been talking throughout this book about opportunity and how we can recreate the culture in our home, in our community, in our nation, in our world. It starts with dreamers. Somebody has to dream a dream. So this book's message is not to politely ask you to dream, but to compel you to realize that we *must* dream for our kids or someone else will dream on their behalf. If we won't dream for them, MTV will dream; BET will dream. If we won't dream, Microsoft will dream. The people that create the most perverted lyrics in the world will dream a dream for our kids. This is not a polite invitation. It is a mandate. If we don't dream, then the future of America and, indeed, the future of the one billion teenagers of the world lie in the hands of those who would dream destruction on their behalf.

On the other side of your dream there are young people who are looking for hope, for vision, for direction; they are looking for value and for those who would show and express their value to them. We need to dream not just for the sake of, "Oh, it's really cool to have a dream and do something neat," but for the sake of real live people who are hurting and being destroyed because those who have moral virtue have refused to dream for them. Well, that time has come to an end. You have made it to the end of this book, which means that you must have something inside of you that is compelling you to do something about the future of our youth. So now it's time to take action.

Gather other people together and go through this book with them and begin to dream a dream. Go after the kids in your community. It's time for those who would be the dreamers to stand up and actually be the dreamers. It's time to stop pointing the finger and talking about the morals of this generation and how bad everything is. It's now time to do something about it with a creative expression of God's power through you creating a dream that will capture the heart of a young generation. Together, we can recreate the future for our young people.

ENDNOTES

Introduction

1. Jon Walker, "Family Life Council Says It's Time to Bring Family Back to Life," *Southern Baptist Council*, June 12, 2002. http://www.sbcannualmeeting.net/sbc02/newsroom/news page.asp?ID=261 (accessed May 2008).

Chapter 1: Generation Out of Control

1. "12-Year-Old Beats Toddler to Death with Bat, Police Say." *The Associated Press*, January 6, 2008. http://www.cnn.com/2008/CRIME/01/06/infant.killed.ap/ (accessed May 2008).
2. "Teacher Arrested After Offering Good Grades for Oral Sex," *The Associated Press*, December 21, 2007. http://www.foxnews.com/story/0,2933,317611,00.html (accessed May 2008).
3. Jeremy P. Meyer, "Birth Leave Sought for Girls," *The Denver Post*, January 7, 2008. http://www.denverpost.com/news/ci_7899096 (accessed May 2008).
4. "Colorado Teens Accused of Killing 7-year-old Girl with 'Mortal Kombat' Game Moves," *The Associated Press*, December 20, 2007. http://www.foxnews.com/story/0,2933,317544,00.html (accessed May 2008).
5. "Teen Accused of Trying to Rape a 62-year-old Woman," *ABC2News*, January 10, 2008. http://www.topix.com/editor/profile/abc2news (accessed May 2008).
6. "6th-grade Teacher Gets 10 Years in Prison for Sex with 13-year-old Boy," *The Associated Press*, March 17, 2007. http://www.foxnews.com/story/0,2933,259370,00.html (accessed May 2008).
7. "Mom: Michigan Teen Shooter Stopped Taking Medication Before Killing," *The Associated Press*, March 9, 2007. http://www.foxnews.com/story/0,2933,258023,00.html (accessed May 2008).
8. "Nevada Suspect Arraigned in Case of Videotaped Rape of Girl, 3," *Fox News*, October 17, 2007. http://www.foxnews.com/story/0,2933,302529,00.html (accessed May 2008).
9. "U.S. Prosecutor Accused of Seeking Sex with Girl, 5," *Fox News*, September 18, 2007. http://www.foxnews.com/story/0,2933,297152,00.html (accessed May 2008).
10. "Cops: Texas Girl, 6, Found Hanging in Garage Was Sexually Abused," *Fox News*, September 12, 2007. http://www.foxnews.com/story/0,2933,296585,00.html (accessed May 2008).
11. "Michigan Mom Gets 12 to 22 Years for Sex 'Contract' on Underage Daughter," *The Associated Press*, June 19, 2007. http://www.foxnews.com/story/0,2933,284255,00.html (accessed May 2008).
12. "Man Gets 20 Years for Bizarre Internet Love Triangle Murder," *The Associated Press*, November 27, 2007. http://www.foxnews.com/story/0,2933,313343,00.html (accessed May 2008).
13. "Four College Students Shot Execution-style in Newark, N.J." *The Associated Press*, August 6, 2007. http://www.foxnews.com/story/0,2933,292200,00.html (accessed May 2008).
14. "Young Mother Charged After Her 10-month-old Boy Recorded Sipping Gin and Juice," *The Associated Press*, June 23, 2007. http://www.foxnews.com/story/0,2933,286193,00.html (accessed May 2008).
15. Corey Moss, "Madonna Smooches with Britney and Christina; Justin, Coldplay Win Big at VMAs," *MTV.com*, August 28, 2003. http://www.mtv.com/news/articles/1477729/20030828/spears_britney.jhtml?headlines=true (accessed May 2008).
16. Jeff Leeds, "Spears's Awards Fiasco Stirs Speculation About Her Future," *New York Times*, September 13, 2007. http://www.nytimes.com/2007/09/13/arts/music/13brit.html (accessed May 2008).
17. "Winehouse Dominates Grammys with 5 Wins," *The Associated Press*, February 11, 2008. http://www.msnbc.msn.com/id/23100297/ (accessed May 2008).
18. Veronica Schmidt, "An Amy Winehouse Weekend: From the Police Cells to the Rich List," *Times Online*, April 28, 2008. http://entertainment.timesonline.co.uk/tol/arts_and_enter tainment/music/article3832374.ece.

19. "Annual Estimates of the Population by Sex and Five-Year Age Groups for the United States: April 1, 2000 to July 1, 2007," U.S. Census Bureau. http://www.census.gov/popest/national/asrh/NC-EST2007-sa.html (accessed May 2008).

20. Lauren Ohayon, "I Need It, Mommy!" *That Money Show,* WNET New York. http://www.pbs.org/wnet/moneyshow/cover/111000.html (accessed May 2008).

21. Stefanie Olsen, "Teens and Media: a Full-time Job," *CNET News.com,* December 7, 2006. http://www.news.com/2100-1041_3-6141920.html (accessed May 2008).

22. Douglas Rushkoff, "Merchants of Cool." *Frontline.* http://www.pbs.org/wgbh/pages/frontline/shows/cool/view/ (accessed May 2008).

23. "Viacom Profit Rises on Asset Sale, 'Transformers,'" *Reuters,* November 2, 2007. http://www.cnbc.com/id/21593581/ (accessed May 2008).

Chapter 2: Are We Not Dreamers?

1. "Media Violence," The American Academy of Pediatrics, November 5, 2001, vol. 108, no. 5, pp. 1222-1226. http://aappolicy.aappublications.org/cgi/content/full/pediatrics;108/5/1222 (accessed May 2008).

2. Diane Swanbrow, "Reel Violence," *University of Michigan News,* 2005. http://www.umich.edu/news/research/story/violence.htm (accessed May 2008).

3. "Number of Sexual Scenes on TV Nearly Double Since 1998," The Kaiser Family Foundation, 1998-2005 data. http://www.kff.org/entmedia/entmedia110905nr.cfm (accessed May 2008).

4. Casey Williams, "MTV Smut Peddlers: Targeting Kids with Sex, Drugs, and Alcohol," Parents Television Council, March 2004. http://www.parentstv.org/PTC/publications/reports/mtv2005/main.asp (accessed May 2008).

5. Berry, Sandra H., Rebecca L. Collins, Marc N. Elliot, et al, "Watching Sex on Television Predicts Adolescents Initiation of Sexual Behavior," *Pediatrics,* September 2004, vol. 114, no. 3, pp. e280-e289 http://pediatrics.aappublications.org/cgi/content/full/114/3/e280 (accessed May 2008).

6. Roger Friedman, "No Buyers for Dakota Fanning Rape Movie," *Fox News,* January 25, 2007. http://www.foxnews.com/story/0,2933,246698,00.html (accessed May 2008).

7. Dr. Macenstein, "Bill Gates Spies on His Kids, Limits Internet Access," Macenstein, February 21, 2007. http://macenstein.com/default/archives/538 (accessed May 2008).

8. "Cruise and Spielberg Limit Their Kids' TV Viewing," *Hellomagazine.com,* September 27, 2002. http://www.hellomagazine.com/film/2002/09/27/cruisespielberg (accessed May 2008).

Chapter 3: The Insidious Grip of Culture

1. Judith Kohler, "Colorado Church Gunman Had Been Kicked Out," *Brietbart.com,* December 10, 2007. http://www.breitbart.com/article.php?id=D8TEUPFG0&show_article=1 (accessed May 2008); "Church Gunman Left Online Rant Between Shootings," *Denver News,* December 11, 2007. http://www.thedenverchannel.com/news/14822541/detail.html (accessed May 2008).

2. Lynn Bartels and Carla Crowder, "Fatal Friendship," *Rocky Mountain News,* August 22, 1999. http://denver.rockymountainnews.com/shooting/0822fata1.shtml (accessed May 2008).

3. "Jamie Lynn Spears Biography (1991-)," Biography.com. http://www.biography.com/search/article.do?id=262390&page=print

4. Ben Thompson, "Tell Us Your Story," *Honor Academy Intern,* January 2008.

Chapter 4: How We Let the Culture into Our Homes

1. David Walsh, Ph.D., "Video Game Violence and Public Policy," paper presented at Playing by the Rules: The Cultural Policy Challenges of Video Games, October 26-27, 2001, Chicago, Illinois. http://culturalpolicy.uchicago.edu/conf2001/papers/walsh.html (accessed May 2008).

2. Mary A. Hepburn, "Violence in Audio-visual Media: How Educators Can Respond," *ERIC* Digest, April 2001. http://www.ericdigests.org/2001-4/violence.html (accessed May 2008).

3. Walsh, "Video Game Violence and Public Policy."

4. Glenn Chapman, "U.S. Video Game Sales Soar to Record 17.9 Billion Dollars," AFP, January 19, 2008. http://afp.google.com/article/ALeqM5jH1jm0BaYBUspP7YByrHm_hPsGUw (accessed May 2008).

5. Linda S. Mintle, Ph.D., "Exposure to Violent Video Games Can Increase Aggressive Behavior," *Charisma*, from a study conducted in 1998 involving Sega and Nintendo video games.

6. Jeremiah Owyang, "Social Network Stats: Facebook, MySpace, Reunion," Web Strategy by Jeremiah, January 2008. http://www.web-strategist.com/blog/2008/01/09/social-network-stats-facebook-myspace-reunion-jan-2008/ (accessed May 2008); Alex Moskalyuk, "Age Demographics of MySpace Visitors," IT Facts, ZDNet, October 30, 2006. http://blogs.zdnet.com/ITFacts/?p=11967 (accessed May 2008).

7. "Press Room: Statistics," Facebook.com, 2008. http://www.facebook.com/press/info.php?statistics (accessed May 2008); Andrew Lipsman, "Facebook Sees Flood of New Traffic from Teenagers and Adults," ComScore, July 5, 2007 (data from May 2007). http://www.comscore.com/press/release.asp?press=1519 (accessed May 2008).

8. "You're 15: Who's Watching You Online?" *CBS News*, June 14, 2006. http://www.cbsnews.com/stories/2006/06/08/gentech/main1696408.shtml?source=RSS&attr=_1696408 (accessed May 2008).

9. "Report: Feds Probe Internet Suicide," *San Francisco Chronicle*, January 9, 2008. http://www.sfgate.com/cgi-bin/article.cgi?f=/n/a/2008/01/08/national/a171155S85.DTL&type=politics (accessed May 2008).

10. Christy Oglesby, "Cells, Texting Give Predators Secret Path to Kids," *CNN.com*, January 11, 2008. http://www.cnn.com/2008/CRIME/01/11/teachers.charged/ (accessed May 2008).

11. "Pornography and Sadistic Violence," Pro-Life: Promoting a Culture of Life, data based on Nielsen TV Rating Service Study. http://www.prolife.org.ph/filemanager/download/45/Pornography_and_Sadistic_violence.pdf (accessed May 2008).

12. "Children and Media Facts," National Institute on Media and the Family. http://www.mediafamily.org/facts/facts.shtml (accessed May 2008); "'Media Multi-tasking' Changing the Amount of Nature of Young People's Media Use," The Henry J. Kaiser Family Foundation. March 9, 2005, http://www.kff.org/entmedia/entmedia030905nr.cfm (accessed May 2008).

Chapter 5: A Cultural Dashboard for Your Family

1. "Internet Pornography Statistics," My Kids Browser, LLC. http://www.mykidsbrowser.com/internet-pornography-statistics.php (accessed May 2008).

2. Margaret Webb Pressler, "For Texting Teens, an OMG Moment When the Phone Bill Arrives," *Washington Post*, May 20, 2007. http://www.washingtonpost.com/wp-dyn/content/article/2007/05/19/AR2007051901284.html (accessed May 2008).

3. Michael Rubinkam, "Cell Phone Porn Scandal Hits U.S. School," *The Associated Press*, January 25, 2008. http://www.msnbc.msn.com/id/22840727/ (accessed May 2008).

4. "Cops: High School Students Traded Nude Pics of Themselves over Cell Phones," *The Associated Press*, January 16, 2008. http://www.foxnews.com/story/0,2933,323373,00.html (accessed May 2008).

5. "Trading Nude Photos Via Mobile Phone Now Part of Teen Dating, Experts Say," *The Associated Press*, Monday April 14, 2008. http://www.foxnews.com/story/0,2933,351171,00.html (accessed May 2008).

6. "AT&T Smart Limits™," AT&T. http://www.att.com/gen/sites/smartlimits?pid=8938 (accessed May 2008).

7. Dionne Searcey, "Keeping Junior on a Wireless Leash," *Washington Post*, September 4, 2007. http://online.wsj.com/article/SB118886181929516309.html?mod=googlenews_wsj (accessed May 2008).

Chapter 6: Convenient Parenting = Brainwashed Kids

1. "Dual Income: Blessing or Curse?" Marriage—Families, June 17, 2006. http://marriage.families.com/blog/dual-income-blessing-or-curse (accessed May 2008).

2. Arnaud De Borchgrave, "Time for TV Detox," *United Press International,* March 5, 2007. http://www.terradaily.com/reports/Time_For_TV_Detox_999.html (accessed May 2008); Stefanie Olsen, "Teens and Media: A Full-Time Job," *CNET News.com,* December 7, 2006. http://www.news.com/Teens-and-media-a-full-time-job/2100-1041_3-6141920.html (accessed May 2008).

Chapter 7: Who Owns Their Heart?
1. Lena Bluestein, "A Generation Impacted Equals a Country Changed," Definitiv by Lena Bluestein, April 29 2006. http://www.lenabluestein.com/blogs/2006/04/a_generation_im.html (accessed May 2008).

Chapter 8: Windows to the Heart
1. "Depression: Suicide Warning Signs," International Still's Disease Foundation. http://www.stillsdisease.org/related_diseases/depression (accessed May 2008).
2. "Why Young People Join Gangs and What You Can Do," Violence Prevention Institute, Inc. http://www.violencepreventioninstitute.org/youngpeople.html (accessed May 2008).

Chapter 9: Communicating Your Values
1. Joseph A. D'Agostino, "Hollywood Makes 'R' Movies, While 'G' Movies Makes Money," FindArticles.com, March 5, 1999. http://findarticles.com/p/articles/mi_qa3827/is_199903/ai_n8848353 (accessed May 2008).
2. "A good name is more desirable than great riches; to be esteemed is better than silver or gold" (Prov. 22:1, *NIV*).

Chapter 11: A Strong Marriage = Secure Kids
1. Glenn T. Stanton, "Defending Marriage: Debate-Tested Sound Bites," Focus on the Family. http://www.family.org/socialissues/A000001140.cfm (accessed May 2008).
2. Jonathan M. Honeycutt, Ph.D (c), M.P.A., M.A., I.P.C., "Ninety Percent of Divorced Fathers Have Less than Full Custody of Their Children," Center for Children's Justice, Inc. http://www.childrensjustice.org/stats.htm (accessed May 2008).

Chapter 12: No Substitute for One on One
1. D'Vera Cohn, "Do Parents Spend Enough Time with Their Children?" Population Reference Bureau, January 2007. http://www.prb.org/Articles/2007/DoParentsSpendEnoughTimeWithTheirChildren.aspx (accessed May 2008).
2. David C. Atkins and Andrew Christensen, "Is Professional Training Worth the Bother? A Review of the Impact of Psychotherapy Training on Client Outcome," *Australian Psychologist* 36, no. 2 (July 2001): 122-130.

Chapter 14: Show Me Da Money, and I'll Show You What You Value
1. Teresa McEntire, "How Much Do You Spend on Christmas?" Families.com, LLC, November 17, 2006. http://parenting.families.com/blog/how-much-do-you-spend-on-christmas (accessed May 2008).

Chapter 16: One Generation Away from Extinction
1. "Most Twentysomethings Put Christianity on the Shelf Following Spiritually Active Teen Years," The Barna Group, Ltd., September 11, 2006. http://www.barna.org/FlexPage.aspx?Page=BarnaUpdate&BarnaUpdateID=245 (accessed May 2008).
2. "American Church Research Project: Surprising Stats in New Church Research—Nationwide Church Attendance Less than Half of Previous Estimates," NewNE.net, October 12, 2006. http://leondejuda.org/db_public/u14_public/index_EN.php?display=onepage&what=1578 (accessed May 2008).
3. "Church Attendance," The Barna Group, Ltd. http://www.barna.org/FlexPage.aspx?Page=Topic&TopicID=10 (accessed May 2008).

4. David T. Olson, "The State of the American Church Powerpoint, Slide 19," The American Church Research Project, 2006. See the powerpoint presentation at http://theameri canchurch.org/.
5. Win Arn, *The Pastor's Manual for Effective Ministry* (Monrovia, CA: Church Growth, 1988), p. 41.
6. John Jalsevac, "The World's 'Most Dangerous' Spiritual Guru: Oprah Begins 10-Week Online New Age Class," *Life Site News,* March 7, 2008. http://www.lifesitenews.com/ldn/printer-friendly.html?articleid=08030701 (accessed May 2008); "The Church of Oprah Exposed," YouTube, LLC, March 26, 2008. http://youtube.com/watch?v=JW4LLwkgmqA&feature=re lated (accessed May 2008).
7. "Saved! (2004)," IMDb.com, Inc. http://www.imdb.com/title/tt0332375/ (accessed May 2008).
8. "German Politician Has Cure for 7-Year Itch," *RTÉ Commercial Enterprises Limited,* September 20, 2007. http://www.rte.ie/news/2007/0920/marriage.html (accessed May 2008).
9. "Erdogan Slams Newspapers for Publishing Pictures of 'Naked Women' Photos," *The Associated Press,* February 13, 2008. http://www.hurriyet.com.tr/english/8224145.asp?gid= 74&sz=32297 (accessed May 2008).
10. Paul Belien, "Jihad: It's About Abortion and Gays, Stupid! Or Isn't It?" *The Brussels Journal,* March 16, 2006. http://www.brusselsjournal.com/node/918 (accessed May 2008).
11. "Naked News Media Advisory: Naked News Moves on Europe," PR Newswire Europe, Ltd., August 5, 2007. http://www.prnewswire.co.uk/cgi/news/release?id=127868 (accessed May 2008).
12. Tom Lowry, "Can MTV Stay Cool?" The McGraw-Hill Companies Inc., February 20, 2006. http://www.businessweek.com/magazine/content/06_08/b3972001.htm (accessed May 2008).
13. "Evangelism Is Most Effective Among Kids," The Barna Group, Ltd., October 11, 2004. http://www.barna.org/FlexPage.aspx?Page=BarnaUpdate&BarnaUpdateID=172 (accessed May 2008).

Chapter 17: Creating a Church Where Teens *Want* to Come

1. Jon Walker, "Council Says It's Time to Bring Family Back to Life," Southern Baptist Convention, June 12, 2002. http://www.sbcannualmeeting.net/sbc02/newsroom/newspage. asp?ID=261 (accessed May 2008).
2. Dave Earley, "The Desperate Need for New Churches," Liberty University, July 17, 2006. http://209.85.141.104/search?q=cache:cZ4GFhpdTxoJ:https://www.liberty.edu/media/ 1162/cmt/The%2520Desperate%2520Need%2520for%2520New%2520Churches%25202%25 20page.doc+Bill+Easum,+%E2%80%9CThe+Easum+Report&hl=en&ct=clnk&cd=2&gl=us (accessed May 2008).
3. "Resources: Marketing to Kids," CBS Interactive, Inc., May 17, 2007. http://www.cbsnews .com/stories/2007/05/14/fyi/main2798401.shtml (accessed May 2008).

Chapter 18: Dreamers for God

1. Anna Carugati, "Interviews: Bill Roedy," WSN Inc., October 2007. http://www.world screen.com/interviewscurrent.php?filename=Roedy1007.htm (accessed May 2008).
2. See The Dream Center at www.dreamcenter.org.
3. "Jonathan said to his young armor-bearer, 'Come, let's go over to the outpost of those uncircumcised fellows. Perhaps the LORD will act in our behalf. Nothing can hinder the LORD from saving, whether by many or by few'" (1 Sam. 14:6, *NIV*).
4. "His preaching will turn the hearts of fathers to their children, and the hearts of children to their fathers" (Mal. 4:6, *NLT*).

Chapter 19: Anatomy of a NextGen Church

1. "State of American Teens," BattleCry.com. http://www.battlecry.com/files/NYAM/Youth %20Awareness%20Sunday%20Powerpoint.ppt (accessed May 2008).
2. See Hillsong Church at www2.hillsong.com.

3. See Prestonwood Baptist Church website at www.prestonwood.org.
4. See New Life Church at www.newlifechurch.org.
5. See Bethany World Prayer Center at http://www.bethany.com/ (accessed May 2008).
6. See Fellowship Church at www.fellowshipchurch.com.
7. See The City Church at http://www.thecity.org.
8. Joanie Aprill, "Tell Us Your Story," *Honor Academy Graduate Intern*, August School of Worship 2007-2008, January 9, 2008.
9. Sarah Neumann, "Tell Us Your Story," *Honor Academy Intern*, January 2008, January 9, 2008.
10. Sarah Garnett, "Tell Us Your Story," *Honor Academy Intern*, August 2007-2008, January 9, 2008.

Chapter 20: Churches that Break the Mold: Double Vision Stories
1. "Cool Conversations/Interviews: Interview with Jim Burns," The Source for Youth Ministries, July 11, 2000. http://www.thesource4ym.com/interviews/jimburns.asp (accessed May 2008).

Chapter 21: Dreamers Always Win (the Culture War)
1. "The Big Five of Commercial Media," World-Information.org. http://world-information.org/wio/infostructure/100437611795/100438659010 (accessed May 2008).
2. Laurie Goodstein, "Evangelicals Fear the Loss of Their Teenagers," *New York Times,* October 6, 2006. http://www.nytimes.com/2006/10/06/us/06evangelical.html?_r=1&sq=Ron%20Luce&st=nyt&adxnnl=1&oref=slogin&scp=4&adxnnlx=1209582050-VudW4yeTjRmHr3NjBDsqcQ (accessed May 2008).

Chapter 22: Paralyzed by the Ordinary
1. "More on the Britney-Madonna Kiss!" *The Associated Press,* September 5, 2003. http://www.cbsnews.com/stories/2003/09/05/entertainment/main571865.shtml (accessed May 2008).

Chapter 23: Winning the PR War
1. Nicole Geary, "Local Teens Rally for Their Generation," *Lansing State Journal,* May 12, 2006. http://www.wzzm13.com/news/news_article.aspx?storyid=54336 (accessed May 2008).
2. "Teens in Cape Girardeau Protest Sex and Violence in Media," *Southeast Missourian*, May 13, 2006. http://medialab.semissourian.com/story/1152572 (accessed May 2008).
3. Deborah Sederberg, "Church Protests Sex, Violence in Media," *The News-Dispatch*, May 13, 2006. http://nl.newsbank.com/nl-search/we/Archives (accessed May 2008).
4. "Teens Spurn Negative Values, Farmington Group's Rally Decries Drink, Drugs, Sex," *The Detroit News*, May 13, 2006. http://nl.newsbank.com/nl-search/we/Archives (accessed May 2008).
5. Ryan Myers, "Teens Seeking Morality Gather for 'BattleCry,' " *Midland Reporter-Telegram*, May 10, 2006. http://nl.newsbank.com/nl-search/we/Archives (accessed May 2008).
6. Kristin E. Holmes, "Teen Crusade: Tune Out, Not In, A Christian Group Comes to Town with a Message on Pop Culture," *The Philadelphia Inquirer,* May 13, 2006. http://nl.newsbank.com/nl-search/we/Archives (accessed May 2008).
7. Stephanie Martin, "City Condemns 'BattleCry' Youth Rally," Group Publishing, Inc., July/August 2006. http://findarticles.com/p/articles/mi_qa3835/is_200607/ai_n17181262 (accessed May 2008).
8. David Kinnaman and Gabe Lyons, *unChristian* (Grand Rapids, MI: Baker Books, 2007).
9. "The 1972 Gay Rights Platform." http://www.article8.org/docs/general/platform.htm (accessed May 2008).
10. Michael Swift, "Gay Revolutionary," *Gay Community News*, February 15-21, 1987. http://www.fordham.edu/halsall/pwh/swift1.html (accessed May 2008).
11. David A. Wyatt, "Gay/Lesbian/Bisexual Television Characters," May 9, 2008. http://home.cc.umanitoba.ca/~wyatt/tv-char2000s.html#test104 (accessed May 2008).
12. "'Mom' and 'Dad' Banished by California," *WorldNetDaily.com Inc.*, October 13, 2007. http://www.worldnetdaily.com/news/article.asp?ARTICLE_ID=58130 (accessed May 2008).

13. Rosamund Elwin and Michele Paulse, illustrated by Dawn Lee, *Asha's Mums* (Toronto, ON: Women's Press, 1990).

14. Taylor Gandossy, "Gay Adoption: A New Take on the American Family," *CNN.com,* June 27, 2007. http://www.cnn.com/2007/US/06/25/gay.adoption/index.html (accessed May 2008).

15. "COLAGEr Question for Presidential Candidates," YouTube, LLC, August 13, 2007. http://youtube.com/watch?v=DTk6Fjr3ycI (accessed May 2008).

16. Bob Unruh, "'Five Pillars of Islam' Taught in Public School," *WorldNetDaily.com Inc.,* October 10, 2006. http://www.worldnetdaily.com/news/article.asp?ARTICLE_ID=52335 (accessed May 2008).

17. Noreen S. Ahmed-Ullah, Sam Roe and Laurie Cohen, "A Rare Look at Secretive Brotherhood in America," *Chicago Tribune,* September 19, 2004. http://www.chicagotribune.com/news/specials/chi-0409190261sep19,1,3910166.story (accessed May 2008).

18. Dr. Anis Shorrosh, D.Min., D.Phil., "Twenty-Year Plan for USA: Islam Targets America," December 2002. http://www.islam-in-focus.com/Press%20Release%20Christmas%202002.htm (accessed May 2008).

19. Seth Mydans, "U.S. Fears Islamic Militancy Could Emerge in Cambodia," *New York Times,* December 22, 2002. http://query.nytimes.com/gst/fullpage.html?res=9903E0DA163CF931A15751C1A9649C8B63 (accessed May 2008).

20. "Number of Muslims in the United States," Adherents.com. http://www.adherents.com/largecom/com_islam_usa.html (accessed May 2008).

Chapter 24: Who Told Us to Shut Up?

1. Ken Anderson, "Overview of Bible Study: The Blood of the Martyrs." http://kenanderson.net/bible/html/martyrs.html (accessed May 2008).

2. "They had such a sharp disagreement that they parted company. Barnabas took Mark and sailed for Cyprus, but Paul chose Silas and left, commended by the brothers to the grace of the Lord. He went through Syria and Cilicia, strengthening the churches" (Acts 15:39-42).

3. "Michelangelo: Art for Faith's Sake," *Christianity History & Biography* 91, (2006). http://www.christianhistorystore.com/ch91michelangelo.html (accessed May 2008).

4. "George Frideric Handel," *Today's Christian* 39, no. 6, (2001): 15. http://www.christianitytoday.com/tc/ 2001/006/9.15.html (accessed May 2008).

5. "Testing the Faith: 'Gay Pride' Features Simulated Sex, Attacking 'Mob,'" *WorldNetDaily.com Inc.,* June 14, 2005. http://www.worldnetdaily.com/news/article.asp?ARTICLE_ID=44753 (accessed May 2008).

6. Shaunti Feldhahn, "Are Schools Encouraging Students to Have Sex?" *Atlanta Journal-Constitution,* October 27, 2007. http://www.ajc.com/blogs/content/shared-blogs/ajc/woman/entries/2007/10/27/index.html (accessed May 2008).

Chapter 26: Teens Who Are Changing Their Generation

1. "Youth Group Protests Store's 'Pornaments,'" *News4Jax.com,* December 6, 2006. http://www.news4jax.com/news/10479455/detail.html (accessed May 2008).

2. "Top Ten Facts About Modern Slavery," Free the Slaves, 2007. http://www.freetheslaves.net/NETCOMMUNITY/Page.aspx?pid=375&srcid=424 (accessed May 2008).

3. Jana Riess, "Abolitionist Teen Speaks Out Against Modern-day Slavery," *Religion BookLine,* February 21, 2007. http://www.publishersweekly.com/article/CA6418085.html (accessed May 2008); Interviews with Zack can be found at www.myspace.com/lc2lc (accessed May 2008).

4. "Mayor Michael Sessions," City of Hillsdale. http://www.ci.hillsdale.mi.us/sessions.htm (accessed May 2008).

5. Jordan Kintner "Tell Us Your Story," *Honor Academy Intern,* August 2007-2008.

6. Brianna Keleher, "Tell Us Your Story," *Honor Academy Intern,* January 2008.

ACKNOWLEDGMENTS

Life gives us many seasons. And as each one ends and a new one begins, one realizes that the only thing that is constant and stable is the love of a faithful God.

I started a journey more than 22 years ago with nothing in front of me but the dreams and hopes of a heart desperate for change. However, I did have beside me a loyal friend who loved me and believed in me enough to walk in obedience toward a calling that continues to daily be defined. Her steadfast trust is what motivates me to also trust in a hope that one day a new reality will be the reality I dream of for our children. Thank you, Katie, for your quiet strength, because without it I would never have been able to dream God's dream of changing the world by reaching a generation, much less build a foundation in our home. It is because of that foundation that I am grateful enough to appreciate the sacrifices that my children have selflessly given time and time again. Hannah, Charity and Cameron—I never realized that one of the greatest blessings I could ever experience as a father would be to catch the vision that you each now cast for me.

I have also learned with each new season that nothing great can be accomplished alone. Behind every success is a countless army of talent who willingly remain hidden in the shadows so that their talents may be used to benefit a cause greater than themselves. Teen Mania Ministries has a rich history because of the dedicated lives who have come and gone and even come again. True loyalty is a gift that is so priceless it is humbling. Thank you, Charity, for faithfully editing and adding your own young perspective to each chapter. You are a precious young woman and a great example for your generation of using your God-given gifts to change the world. One of the greatest things about this book was working on it together with you. Thank you,

ACKNOWLEDGMENTS

Rebekah Morris, Beth King, Becky Burnham, Meredith Ambrose, Michelle Janke, Simone Nickel, Rachel Burrow and Christina Bourassa, for the many hours of research and editing. Thank you, Idalia Saravia, Sarah Tagaloa and Michelle Mavridis, for jumping in to help type out all my thoughts. Thank you, Kevin Benson, for your help, support and, most importantly, your friendship.

Ron Luce

Teen Mania's Mission Statement:

To provoke a young generation to passionately pursue Jesus Christ and to take His life-giving message to the ends of the earth!

Aquire the Fire
BattleCry
CCM
Global Expeditions
Honor Academy
Local Church Partnerships

www.teenmania.org